The Irish Property Buyers' Handbook 2012/2013

ABOUT THE AUTHOR

Carol Tallon has been managing director of Buyers Broker Ltd., Ireland's only property buyers' agency franchise, since 2006. Well-known for her regular media and radio features as the Irish property buyers' champion, Carol was the property writer for *Propertywise* magazine and continues to contribute to national and local press. Together with the team at Buyers Broker Ltd., she delivers property seminars and auction training on a regular basis throughout the year. Carol can be contacted on caroltallon@buyersbroker.ie.

GUEST CONTRIBUTOR

Karl Deeter is a native of Los Angeles and one of Ireland's best-known commentators in mortgages and personal finance. He is a regular contributor on all of the national media. As a Qualified Financial Advisor, he holds a Mortgage Diploma, a certificate in Compliance, and attended Dublin Institute of Technology where he obtained a certificate and diploma in management. He is currently working his way through the ACCA exams, while also studying Islamic Finance through the Chartered Institute of Securities & Investments in London.

As operations manager of Irish Mortgage Brokers since 2004 and a director of Trinity Accountants, auditors and financial advisors, he spends every working hour on the topic of finance, financial planning and taxation. The little spare time left is spent with his wife and family or playing bluegrass music.

THE IRISH PROPERTY BUYER'S HANDBOOK 2012/2013

Carol Tallon

Published by OAK TREE PRESS
19 Rutland Street, Cork, Ireland
www.oaktreepress.com

A catalogue record of this book is available from the British Library.

ISBN 978 1 78119 040 1 (Paperback)
ISBN 978 1 78119 041 8 (ePub)
ISBN 978 1 78119 042 5 (Kindle)

The information contained in this publication is intended for
guideline purposes only and does not represent legal advice.
Readers should always seek independent legal and/or other
professional advice specific to their own requirements before
taking any action based on the information provided herein.

CONTENTS

ACKNOWLEDGEMENTS

I would like to thank the team at Buyers Broker Ltd., in particular my long suffering business partner, Orla Fitzmaurice, for their continued and much appreciated support. There are so many people who contributed to this book in some form or other, like the estate agents who opened my eyes to hidden gems, or the mortgage brokers who kept me updated on lender trends, or my very good friends who understood that good coffee is the hallmark of any successful endeavour! I would especially like to thank my publisher, Brian O'Kane, and his team at Oak Tree Press, for allowing me to twist his arm just a little! Finally, I would especially like to thank all of the property buyers who dared to challenge the traditional model of buying and selling property in Ireland, which made my role within the industry possible. I look forward to disrupting the industry for many years to come.

DEDICATION

This book is dedicated to my beautiful daughter Katie and to my parents Sean and Kathleen Tallon, my silent partners in this and every endeavour.

Chapter 1

THE ECONOMIC OUTLOOK

Where are we now?

2011 was another tough year for the Irish property market. Property prices fell for the fifth consecutive year. Recorded drops for 2011 were 15 to 17 per cent, depending upon which source is to be believed, though none are entirely accurate. It is difficult to assess the average drop in prices since the boom years with any degree of accuracy because of the lack of available house price data; however, it now appears to be in the 50 to 60 per cent range. This is causing hardship for existing homeowners who find themselves in negative equity. The painful reality is that it is in the national interest to have realistic and sustainable property prices. In order to achieve this, property prices needed to come down to more realistic levels. Essentially, for a property market to function, working members of society need to be able to buy their own homes. From the periods 2001 to 2006/7, this was simply not an option for many of the young, working families starting out.

Property markets tend to operate as cycles. In the UK, this cycle tends to be 10 years. Historically in Ireland, the cycle tended to shorter, with property doubling in value every seven years. As shown in **Figure 1.1**, in the decade from 1996 to 2006, property did not double, but rather increased by between 260 per cent to almost 400 per cent nationwide. This was unsustainable and a crash was inevitable. Whilst property prices were expected to fall, they were certainly not expected to go into meltdown. Most commentators acknowledged the bubble; what was not anticipated was the further political turmoil, continuing banking scandals and the sheer scale of the International Monetary Fund(IMF)/EU bailout.

Figure 1.1: Percentage House Price Change 1996-2006

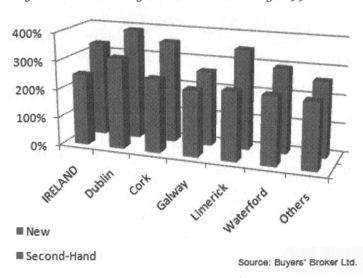

There are almost daily commentaries from professionals and non-professionals alike, some calling the bottom of the market and other extremists lamenting that we may not see it for another generation. Based on experiences working on the ground, the writer finds that there is no single answer; the 'market' is comprised of hundreds of local markets and those local markets do not behave in a uniform manner. Certainly, the market as a whole does not appear to have levelled out but the widely-accepted position is that the property market looks closer to stabilising now than it did in early 2010 and the process of stabilisation appears to have started in 2011.

Many would-be property buyers will have some difficulty with that statement and they would be right. It is much too simplistic a view of such a hugely complex market. In Ireland, there is no single national property market. For such a relatively small geographical area, there is a huge variance in terms of neighbourhoods and property type; therefore, even taking a regional view will be largely irrelevant or inaccurate. In reality, the market is far more unruly than people appreciate. Prices in Kildare will not magically rectify themselves just because Wicklow sellers finally got real. There will be no welcome signpost announcing the market's arrival at the bottom; in fact, most buyers will drive through this one-horse town without even slowing down, because the bottom in any given area will not become apparent for at least three to four months. By the time this news is broadcast, prices have started to lift, motivated sellers are less motivated to accept lower offers and the window of opportunity starts to gradually shrink. This can be seen more clearly in concentrated pockets around the country. For the foreseeable future, local is where it's at for would-be buyers.

The best advice for buyers in such an uncertain market is to stop looking at general statistics (national or regional), and instead to research then interrogate their local specifics. For example, three bedroom houses in Blackrock, South County Dublin hit their lowest price in the summer and early autumn of 2009 and have been recovering ever since, whereas neighbouring Stilorgan was a good nine to 12 months behind this trend due to a higher supply of houses. Stilorgan, Dundrum and the surrounding areas are now experiencing a shortage of quality three and four bedroom houses, while apartments in the locality continue to plummet. For buyers researching this particular area in South County Dublin, this distinction will not be made clear and resulting decisions will be made using flawed data. This situation arises in every single area around Ireland. In the capital, the average house price plunged 17 per cent from a year earlier in 2011. Areas outside Dublin were also badly hit, with the average price 14 per cent down over the same period. For this reason, ~~it is essential to research on an extremely local level to ensure value.~~

There can be no doubt that property was no longer sexy or fashionable in 2011, but for many, it remained and continues to be a natural fact of life. As time moves on, life continues. People graduate, start their careers, get promoted. Relationships form, progress and evolve. Homes are necessary; renting is rarely cost-efficient or satisfying beyond early adulthood. Ireland has a culture of homeownership that transcends economic forecasts and fear-mongering. Our collective need to acquire land has driven us to favour houses over apartments, regardless of how plush that apartment might be. ~~Logical reasoning suggests~~ that land, ~~however small the plot, will always be more valuable than~~ a legal ~~interest over land. Irish~~ home-owners have not yet have embraced ~~apartment living~~ and this is supported by the diminishing stock of three bedroom houses in areas of high first-time buyer demand, whereas the stock of available apartments continues to rise in line with completions. As the stock of available houses runs low, this theory will be tested. It is expected that apartments will be acceptable only after houses have risen beyond the budgets of homebuyers and, given the level of oversupply with apartments nationwide, this will likely take a period of years, not months.

Supply and Demand

Traditionally, residential demand in Ireland was for approximately 40,000 homes a year. During the boom years, new units constructed reached an unfathomable 90,000 annually. According to Homebond, a mere 1,680 new homes were registered in 2010 (3,337 in 2009). This is positive in the short term, particularly as there is no longer any incentive to buy a newly-built property, but it is positive only if the stall in construction is temporary. Future construction then must be in line with proven demand, not just in terms of volume but more critically, property type. There has been a notable lack of planning or, more accurately, misguided planning in this country, particularly in urban centres, which has led to a skewed demand/supply model – resulting in an excess of apartments rather than houses irrespective of buyer preferences.

Simply put, as a nation, we Irish did not build homes that fulfilled the needs and desires of home-buyers. As already mentioned, Irish home-buyers, and to a certain extent investors, favour houses to apartments. There are many reasons for this, practical, historical and cultural. This is unlikely to change in the short term but innovative professionals are trying to come up with creative solutions to marry the differences going forward.

What can Buyers Expect in 2012/2013?

It was a busy start to the year, with the first three property reports of 2012 released in early January. These reports came from daft.ie, myhome.ie and the Central Statistics Office (CSO). While there was some contradictory reporting, due to the lack of real data, the general trajectory was negative. To recap, daft.ie suggested that the asking prices for houses are now 52 per cent below the peak, showing an 18 per cent fall in 2011 alone, whereas myhome.ie suggested that asking prices are only 43 per cent down. This will no doubt confuse buyers, who read about 50 per cent decreases back in 2010 or apartment owners who are reducing their offering by 70 per cent and still failing to find a buyer. So what is going on?

In addition to looking at the rental market, which is a key indicator of property values, several leading economists also have examined current levels of employment, income, and inflation. All of these findings lean towards further declines of property generally throughout 2012 and some, most notably Ronan Lyons, have been criticised for saying that falling house prices are not necessarily a bad thing as they get house prices back to where they should be based on fundamental economic conditions.

The daft.ie report is definitely the most comprehensive in terms of area and property type breakdowns; however, buyers ought to bear in mind that this report, however comprehensive, is based on 'asking prices' of daft.ie users – it is not, and cannot be used as, a definitive database of prices – it is an indicator, at best.

In relation to mortgage information, the latest CSO report shows that a mere 13,000 mortgages were issued in 2011, down almost 95 per cent from peak figures. 2012 is already shaping up to be a better year for mortgaged homebuyers, with €1.5 billion of mortgage credit pledged by Bank of Ireland. The laws of competition mean that AIB and PTSB are likely to follow suit if they can. ECB interest rates are currently at 1 per cent levels and the general feeling is that they will remain low for much of 2012, with slight increases in 2013.

Looking at income, employment, taxes, economic outlooks for Ireland, Europe and the world has economists running scared of property and it continually stumps them that purchases continue. Stale stock, or properties on the market for period in excess of a year, has led to increased off-market purchases in the residential and commercial market; this is not a usual reaction. The lack of credit has led to increased cash purchases; however, with poor home-buyer sentiment outside the capital, buyer trends remain difficult to predict. Although unemployment, at just over 14 percent, remains high, Q1 of 2012 saw the first growth in employment figures since 2007. This must be seen as a positive development.

It is well-established that quality properties, generally three or four bedroom houses, in desirable, residential areas are well into their recovery. For other properties, so-called recovery will not come. As a nation, Ireland built a volume of inferior homes, or homes where buyers simply do not wish to live. Consequently, the only way recovery nationwide will happen is when bulldozers take the places of the nation's repossessed cranes.

The most important message that buyers need to hear is that there is an opportunity to buy well in any market. A cheap property can be bought cheaply at any time. The key to buying well is to seek value at prices that are well below market values. Buyers in 2012 will need to be sure of their requirements, both in the immediate and in the longer term. The concept of a starter home is no more; buyers need to understand that any property purchases should suit their needs in the long term.

Budget 2012: Government Initiatives to Stimulate the Property Market

Budget 2012 extended the Tax Relief at Source (TRS) scheme for mortgages slightly. The rate of relief increased to 25 per cent for first-time buyers who buy in 2012, while other home-buyers will receive 15 per cent mortgage interest relief.

Investors will be relieved to learn that tax incentive properties (section 23 and section 50) have retained their reliefs, but only where the investor has an annual income of less than €100,000. Investors with an income greater than €100,000 will be subject to a surcharge of 5 per cent.

While the government stopped short at introducing a property tax (this is expected in Budget 2013, based upon a site value tax), a household charge of €100 has been introduced, with some exemptions for residents living in unfinished housing developments.

Key Interest Rates

Key Eurozone interest rate levels have been low throughout the economic crisis. 2011 saw the return of 1 per cent rates and, at the end of the first quarter of 2012, there is no sign of any increase. In a functioning market, this would be positive news for existing home-owners and prospective home-buyers; however, the property market in Ireland cannot be described as 'functioning'.

Unfortunately for Irish home-owners and buyers, decreased competition in the Irish mortgage market means that lenders have been slow to pass on any decrease to variable rate mortgage holders. At best, current low rates can be seen as European political confidence in the Eurozone economy, despite signs of a slowdown – if a double dip was imminent, the rate no doubt would have seen a slight decrease by now. Slight increases to the ECB interest rate in 2011 were mitigated in early 2012.

National Property Price Register

After many years of petitioning and lobbying from all sectors of property industry, the Minister for Justice, Equality & Defence, Alan Shatter TD and the Irish government finally look likely to introduce an amendment to the *Property Services Bill* so as to establish a National Property Price Register. Both buyers and sellers have been calling for actual house and apartment sale prices to be published officially and it now looks like this could achieved by mid-2012. All indications are that this Register will include actual prices, property addresses and dates of sale.

Prior to the boom years and certainly throughout the 'Tiger sprint', lack of data distorted the market. At the height of the market, this distortion was mainly positive for sellers but negative for buyers. For the last four years, the lack of real, reliable and accurate information has proved negative for both parties as it increased the fear and uncertainty.

The introduction of this Register also means that property valuation system in Ireland finally will become a reliable indicator of real-time, actual residential values. The source of information for the new figures will be the Revenue Commissioners, which gets its information from conveyancing solicitors acting for purchasers.

When implemented, this new register is likely to be a more effective way to stimulate the market than any taxation interest relief for home-buyers as it deals with the domestic market's greatest threat: fear. New and experienced buyers are monitoring the market, afraid to take action. Most will have finance in place or cash reserves that could be used if the right opportunity was to present itself. But there can be no doubt that the uncertainty in the market is preying on the minds of these would-be buyers. When pressed, it appears that buyers are terrified of the financial risk – in particular, the fear paying more than the property is worth and finding they are in negative equity. Significantly, they are afraid of the *appearance* of financial mismanagement and ultimately looking foolish or being ridiculed in the media similar to the way home-buyers and amateur investors who acquired their property during the boom years are now.

The key to motivating buyers to return to the market lies in improving confidence: in the value to be achieved, in the service professionals and most importantly, in the reliability of the available market data.

KEY POINTS FROM CHAPTER 1

- ❖ Ireland's house price boom was one of the longest and biggest in Europe. It saw prices of second-hand homes surge by around 330% from 1996 to 2006.

- ❖ This was effectively a massive bubble, which burst in 2006, to the detriment of most buyers who bought in 2002 to 2006. Prices have now fallen between 50 to 65 per cent from the peak in 2006.

- ❖ All attempts to call the bottom of the market have been unsuccessful; however, most commentators feel the market is stabilising and reaching its trough.

- ❖ There are huge differences in the supply and demand factors around the country; this will lead to disproportionate data reporting so buyers are advised to research their local market.

- ❖ The household charge, a form of property taxation, was introduced in Budget 2012 and is expected to be followed by a site value tax by 2013.

- ❖ The National Property Price Register is expected to be operational in 2012.

Chapter 2

The National Asset Management Agency

What is NAMA and how does it affect buyers?

The National Asset Management Agency (NAMA) is a government initiative that was announced by then Finance Minister Brian Lenihan in the emergency Budget of April 2009 to stabilise the Irish banking system. It was established under the auspices of the National Treasury Management Agency (NTMA) and both agencies are now operating from the Treasury Building (this very building, after a brief legal battle, is now under the control of NAMA). The stated objective of NAMA is:

> *To provide the banks with a clean bill of health, to strengthen their balance sheets, to considerably reduce uncertainty over bed debts and as a consequence ensure the flow of credit on a commercial basis to individuals and businesses in the real economy .*

In real terms, NAMA is the result of an arrangement entered into between the government and certain Irish banks; however, it affects all citizens of Ireland. The central notion behind NAMA was to remove what are referred to as 'toxic loans' from the banks so that their balance sheets improve to the point where they can raise or free up money that, in turn, may be loaned to people and businesses for mortgages and business loans. Essentially, the initiative was to get credit flowing again. At the most basic level,

NAMA was introduced as the solution to the Irish banks' and building societies' extreme over-exposure to property development between 2002 and 2007. The affected banks are: AIB, Bank of Ireland, Anglo Irish Bank and Irish Nationwide. Irish Life & Permanent fell within the remit of the scheme but upon inspection, was not deemed to have loans that qualified for NAMA.

How does NAMA Work?

Existing borrowers, developers for the large part, with loans in Irish banks in excess of €5 million or with loans for property development of any value, have their loans notified to NAMA by their existing lender. NAMA then requests a business plan from each borrower so that it can assess the state of the portfolio and make a decision as to whether the borrower will go forward into the NAMA process. This is entirely NAMA's decision, not the banks'. NAMA is intended to be run as a commercial entity, albeit with any gains accruing to the State after it has run its natural course.

The business model of NAMA is to pay only a portion of what it believes the loan is worth. When we refer to the worth or value of a loan, we are really looking at the security upon which that loan was granted – the properties or development sites that the existing lender holds security for. For example, if the bank advanced a loan for €20 million, NAMA will value the security having regard to a number of key valuation factors and will apply what has been termed in the media as a 'hair cut' to the loan, which essentially means that NAMA is unlikely to pay more than €8 million to €12 million for the loan but will still pursue the borrower for the full extent of the loan (€20 million). In order to do this, NAMA has been granted more extensive powers than the banks in terms of property given as security but it may only pursue the borrower for money under the same terms as the banks advanced the loan initially.

As many developers have since gone into receivership or liquidation, NAMA needs to be in a position to receive a return from the loans acquired from the banks, therefore, it takes over both performing and non-performing loans, much to the dismay of some developers whose portfolios are performing and repayments being made. By this, we can see that the media branding of NAMA as a 'toxic bank' is entirely inaccurate as it is neither toxic (not fully!) nor a bank. Paddy McKillen launched a legal challenge to NAMA to try to keep his portfolio away from it (discussed in detail below). While he was successful on a point of technicality (NAMA acquired the loans prior to the legislation entitling it to do was enacted), the reality remains unchanged and NAMA can legitimately acquire performing assets. This is a positive clarification for the agency – and for the Irish nation – to have received, as the purpose of NAMA is to try to recover as much money for the taxpayer as possible. On that basis, it would simply not make sense for it to acquire only bad loans. The loans to go into NAMA are secured on international properties in addition to the Irish sites and developments. This means that NAMA will get in loans in countries where the property market is out-performing the Irish market, thereby increasing the likelihood of achieving some levels of income and gain for the State.

As mentioned, NAMA will require the borrower to submit a business proposal or plan to assess whether the portfolio is capable of producing an income, be it by way of sale or tenancies. It appears to be the case that NAMA is attempting to work with these borrowers, provided the plan is realistic and based on achievable market projections. It is in the best interests of the borrower to co-operate with the process and make all and any information available to the agency. NAMA has the power to call in their debts and to pursue the borrower directly rather than trying to coax the income from the portfolio; however, it is clear that the options facing NAMA with these properties are to sell, lease, manage, develop, demolish or hold pending an upswing in market conditions over the medium term.

At the time of print, in early 2012, NAMA had acquired property to a 'value' of €72.3 billion at a price of €30.5 billion.

Acquisition value, in this context, was set out in Part 5 of the *NAMA Act* and the *Valuation Regulations*. The reference valuation date for the valuation of all property assets is 30 November 2009.

Paddy McKillen *versus* NAMA

The first legal challenge to NAMA was made by Paddy McKillen to the High Court in July 2010. Mr McKillen, on behalf of 15 of his companies acting as joint applicants, sought to have NAMA's operations and, more particularly, the effects of these operations on his businesses reviewed.

By way of context, Mr. McKillen's companies are estimated to be €2.1bn, representing 2.5 per cent of NAMA's final loans tally. These loans are secured against 62 commercial properties (a mere 2.5 per cent is secured by way of development land) valued somewhere in the region of €1.7 billion to €2.28 billion. According to Mr. McKillen, all of the loan repayments are being met and the annual income generated amounts to €150m, exceeding the interest liabilities. Just over a quarter of the property portfolio is in Ireland, with most of the remainder in the UK, France and the US.

The High Court rejected all points and Mr. McKillen was unsuccessful in his claim and an order for legal costs was made against him. Mr. McKillen exercised his right of appeal, challenging the constitutionality of the legislation. He was granted leave to appeal. The case then was appealed and fast-tracked before the Supreme Court and NAMA agreed to continue the stay on transferring Mr. McKillen's loans pending the outcome of the appeal.

There were five basic points or strands to Mr. McKillen's application as follows:

1. The loans were acquired prior to NAMA being formally established on 21 December 2009.

2. The procedures adopted by NAMA breach his constitutional right to fair procedures.

3. NAMA failed to exercise relevant considerations when judging the inclusion of Mr. McKillen's loans.

4. The loans in question were not/are not so-called 'impaired loans' under the terms of the EC approval.

5. The NAMA legislation fails to define 'eligible loans' adequately to the extent that it renders the Act unconstitutional.

In early February 2011, the Supreme Court ruled that the acquisition by NAMA of Mr. McKillen's loans was not valid as it pre-dated NAMA's formal establishment; however, it was a pyrrhic victory as NAMA subsequently acquired those loans. As discussed above, the Supreme Court also ruled that NAMA is entitled to acquire both performing and non-performing loans, contrary to Mr. McKillen's assertions. Furthermore, the Supreme Court upheld the constitutionality of the *NAMA Act*. It was the first of many legal battles that the agency would undertake in 2011/2012.

NAMA as a Source of Property

It is important for prospective Irish buyers to understand that only 54 per cent of NAMA's entire property portfolio, if it may be deemed that, is situated within the Republic of Ireland. Furthermore, a mere 12 per cent of this stock is made up of residential units for resale. In real terms, the agency now controls an estimated 10,000 completed dwellings nationwide; however, this is likely to increase over the medium term, based upon the extent of undeveloped, or partially-developed, development land held. It will not surprise buyers to learn that 80 per cent of this residential stock is apartments or duplexes.

According to the agency's Chief Executive, Mr. Brendan McDonagh, NAMA is linked to just over one in five unsold newly built residential units across the country. This figure seems low;

however, there does not appear to be any credible data available, outside of NAMA, to prove or disprove these numbers.

NAMA has certainly not been the driving force in the residential market that it was widely expected to be. It is not good enough, either for the State or tax-payers, for NAMA to sit back and wait for the economy to lift the market. The hopes, and financial future, of the nation depends on effective disposal of these assets. NAMA needs to show some early 'wins' for the people of Ireland. It has done this by selling a number of high-profile commercial assets, mainly outside of Ireland. In February 2011, NAMA confirmed the sale of the prestigious Montevetro building, in Dublin 2, to Google for €99.9m. NAMA recently came under pressure when it was accused of selling property through private sales, contrary to its own code of practice, which provides for the sale of assets by way of auction or competitive tendering. For that reason, a teaser action appears to be inevitable at this stage, in addition to other planned impaired asset auctions. It was widely speculated that this would happen in 2011 and it did not. There have been no announcements to date but it does appear likely that 2012/2013 will be the right time for NAMA to focus some energy upon the Irish residential market.

Most importantly, buyers are advised to find out, when dealing with any developer, whether they are part of the NAMA programme because, if they are, that purchase could be subject to the consent of NAMA.

In September 2011, in the context of sourcing property, the author had an opportunity to take part in an RTÉ television *Prime Time* special, entitled *Namaland*. This documentary gave a unique look inside the inner workings of the agency. In it, NAMA's dealings with its debtors/developers were heavily criticised. By way of defence, the same month, NAMA announced that it had agreed the disposal of €4bn of assets. It is expected that NAMA will play a greater role in resuscitating the domestic market in 2012/2013; however, it is likely to be to the benefit of city centre investors rather than home-buyers.

Negative Equity Mortgages

In mid-2011, in response to government and industry critics for failing to address concerns in the domestic residential market, NAMA tentatively announced its negative equity mortgage product (as yet, untitled) to aid first-time buyers who wish to purchase NAMA stock. It will involve the buyer getting a mortgage from one of the pillar banks, but only an agreed portion of the mortgage will be drawn down and paid for the property. The remainder, estimated to be 20 per cent, will be left for a period of time as security against further price drops. In theory, this seems like a good idea. In reality, it puts inexperienced first-time buyers in the position of buying apartments that may not be ideal for medium or long term living. The location of much of this stock is suitable for renting, but perhaps not to start a family in. Buyers should bear in mind that, at some point, most will want to sell or move on and for this to happen, market conditions will need to have improved hugely. Improvement is certainly not a guarantee.

It should be noted here that this is a very different product to the negative equity mortgage scheme recently announced by the pillar banks to help families in negative equity to trade-up, and effectively carry with them the portion of negative equity affecting their current homes.

NAMA as a Source of Social Housing

In 2011, NAMA facilitated the purchase of 57 apartments in Sandyford, Dublin by a voluntary housing association. In early 2012, the agency announced that 2,000 houses and apartments would be made available for social housing. Up to 25 per cent of these units are understood to be located in the Dublin City Council area, with a further 21 per cent in the rest of the county. One-third of the houses and apartments are based in the Cork city and county areas, with the remaining units spread across the country. NAMA offers these properties to local authorities and voluntary housing associations by way of a leasing arrangement, managed by the property owners or receivers, with the option to buy.

This move by NAMA is in direct response to the social housing market, which is recording significantly greater levels of demand and lower levels of supply than other sectors of the market. The Irish Government had previously ruled out the purchase or development of any further local authority housing, citing lack of funds.

This has caused issues for home-buyers who do not wish to buy into a low-occupation estate or development, only to find out that the remaining units have been made available for social tenants. While the official ratio of 20 per cent of social tenants should apply in any apartment block or housing development, NAMA has not ruled out leasing entire blocks of apartments for exclusive social purposes. Buyers will need to bear this in mind if they choose to purchase in such a development.

KEY POINTS FROM CHAPTER 2

- ❖ The stated objective of NAMA is 'To provide the banks with a clean bill of health, to strengthen their balance sheets, to considerably reduce uncertainty over bad debts and as a consequence ensure the flow of credit on a commercial basis to individuals and businesses in the real economy' .

- ❖ NAMA now controls an ever-expanding portfolio of residential and commercial property with an estimated 10,000 residential units nationwide (Q1 2012). Of these units, 80 per cent are thought to be apartments or duplexes (two-storey apartments for our American readers).

- ❖ Buyers are advised to find out, when dealing with any developer, whether they are part of the NAMA programme because if they are, that purchase could be subject to the consent of NAMA.

Chapter 3

DECIDING TO BUY

Is now the right time for you?

The first, and most important, question that any prospective buyer must ask himself is whether now is the right time *for him* to buy. This may be a good time to step into the market – that is, it is undoubtedly a buyer's market – but that does not necessarily mean that it is the right time to invest the time, energy and money in buying a home. Any purchase in this or any market should be for the long term, so it's important to get it right. When a buyer is facing this decision, there are both personal and external market considerations to take into account.

Personal Considerations

1. The first area of consideration is the individual. The prospective buyer must assess genuinely whether he is financially in a position to buy. That means not only whether he will qualify for a mortgage, but also whether he has cash savings of approximately 12 to 13 per cent of the value of the property to put towards the purchase to cover the deposit, stamp duty, legal and agency expenses and other associated costs of buying? If the answer is "No", the prospective buyer would be well advised to consult with a financial adviser who will put together a plan, or financial road map of sorts, to set the buyer on the right track for a successful application in the future. Of course, if the buyer has the cash resources, this is one box ticked; however, being in a position financially still does not mean that it is

necessarily the right time. The prospective home-buyer should evaluate his lifestyle – is he ready to be tied to a mortgage commitment? Another point worthy of consideration is job security; the buyer may have a job today but how secure is his position? Is a career change on the cards, or possibly relocation? All of these factors must be considered before the buyer starts the house-hunting process.

2. The second consideration for the buyer, after he has satisfied himself that he is in a position to start looking for a new home, is the type of property that he requires. Is the buyer in search of a house, an apartment or perhaps a live/work unit that is becoming increasingly popular among first-time buyers? The reason why this is important is that the level of over-supply in the apartment market in some areas is so excessive that buyers might be better served by waiting for the impending bank and NAMA auctions rather than buying now.

3. The third individual consideration is the immediate area in which the buyer is looking. The market as a whole has not levelled out as yet, and is unlikely to do so for another while as the over-hang of apartment stock and poorly appointed new houses continue to distort the market. However, in pockets of the market, where demand from first-time buyers has been high, there was a levelling off in early 2010 and demand remains steady while supply is low and ever-decreasing. Buyers must look to their chosen area and weigh up the local demand *versus* supply or over-supply. Even in areas where property prices may not have hit bottom level, the strategy is not to wait but rather to shop around to find a seller who is willing to reduce their price. Essentially, instead of waiting for the market to drop naturally, the buyer goes ahead with the purchase at below market value (BMV) prices, in anticipation of slight future decreases in the short term – that is, the buyer future-proofs the home.

4. The fourth factor for prospective buyers when considering whether to buy property is fear. Fear is very prevalent in would-be buyers at the moment, but what is interesting is that the fears are different for each buyer. The most common fears are of engaging in the property market as an inexperienced buyer due to a general sense of mistrust; of financial misjudgement resulting in possible negative equity in the future; of further price drops; and interestingly, of missing the opportunity to buy at the bottom of the market. As noted earlier, the lack of available house price data in this country has contributed to this fear for buyers (and sellers as well). These are very real concerns for the buyer and the topic is covered in Chapter 13, 'Valuations', where alternative methods of valuing property are examined with the aim of empowering buyers.

Market Considerations

1. House prices have been falling month-on-month in Ireland since 2007; although the rate of decline has slowed, the direction has been consistent. This is, perhaps, the single greatest concern that buyers have when it comes to entering the market. Many first-time buyers have received mortgage approval in principle (AIP), but are waiting for some media outlet, economist (Ireland's new rock stars!) or market commentator to announce that the bottom of the market has arrived. The bad news for buyers is this is unlikely to happen, and if it does, the announcement is likely to be at least three to six months after the fact due to the delay in data reporting. Buyers will be depending upon mortgage data that is usually three to four months old at the time of issue.

2. Mortgage interest rates are at historically low levels, but despite increases in 2011, the ECB rate returned to just 1% in early 2012. Buyers are likely to face increased mortgage rates if they wait until later in the year before buying. It is worth noting here that the pool of buyers sitting in wait with their AIP will not get

the mortgage rate that they agreed with the lender at the time of approval, but rather the rate determined by the bank on the day the mortgage is drawn down. This means that buyers who are waiting for house prices to hit the floor actually may end up paying more in increased interest repayments.

3. Buyers in 2012 will be entitled to mortgage interest relief at the increased rate of 25 per cent for first-time buyers and 15 per cent for all other home-buyers. This is covered in greater detail in Chapter 5, 'Taxation'.

4. Affordability is the other main market indicator. This is measured by the percentage of net income that is required to service a new mortgage on a monthly basis. This figure now stands at 12.6 per cent, in comparison to the 2006 figure of 26.4 per cent. The most recent report from the EBS/DKM study on affordability shows that buying a property in Ireland has not been as affordable since 1988.

Other Considerations for Investors

1. Access to credit remains difficult for investors, with few lenders open for buy-to-let mortgage business. Those who do secure finance can expect to pay interest rates well in excess of 4 per cent. Some advisers have suggested that investors stress test to a level of 7 per cent.

2. Interest-only mortgages are difficult to negotiate in the current trading environment, and where they are being advanced it is only for a short period of time – certainly no more than a period of three years. Investors will need to be able to demonstrate ability to repay capital and interest.

3. Loan to value (LTV) ratios have gone right down and investors should be prepared to put forward no less than 25 per cent, and possibly up to 50 per cent, cash reserves to purchase the property.

4. Taxation issues and concerns, in particular the controversy surrounding proposed changes to Section 23 properties, are

discussed in greater detail in Chapter 5, 'Tax Implications of Buying Property'.

KEY POINTS FROM CHAPTER 3

❖ Timing is an important factor in buying property but it is not the most important factor. Personal considerations should include the buyer's ability to raise finance, and whether they are in a place in their life where they want the commitment that comes with a home and mortgage.

❖ There is always an opportunity for the buyer to buy well if they research their immediate/local market and shop around for the right seller. When considering the market, buyers should only buy if they can obtain value and verify that value.

❖ The year 2011 was the last one for buyers to qualify for full interest relief on their mortgage interest payment under the TRS scheme. Reduced relief will be available for buyers in 2012.

Chapter 4

BUILDING A PERSONAL PROPERTY TEAM

Get the right advice!

The concept of building a personal property team will be new to most home-buyers. Many are intimidated by the uncertainty in the market as a result of recent economic upheaval, and for some the process is overwhelming. They need help but are unsure what level of help is required or how to go about finding it. Investors, on the other hand, have relied on this type of support and ready access to expertise in the past to build up their portfolios. Their team will have helped them to survive the property market crash with as few wounds as possible.

It is essential for buyers to make a reasoned, well-informed decision about purchasing. If now is the right time for any individual to buy, then access to the most accurate and up-to-date information is crucial, and this does not just apply to first-time buyers. Irrespective of the level of experience that a buyer may have, the market has changed dramatically over the past decade and it continues to change on a weekly and monthly basis. Up-to-date knowledge, industry insights and access to property professionals help buyers to navigate the buying process effectively. No buyer can afford to buy poorly in the current market – or, indeed, in any market.

So what is a personal property team? This will vary from one buyer to the next, depending upon their experience in the market, knowledge of the industry, levels of capability and expectations.

The team is basically a circle of expert advisers that a buyer can rely on. There are no group meetings or formal set-up. It is not necessary that the various professionals know each other or are in contact with each other; however, sometimes one will be referred by another and a good working relationship between them might benefit the buyer further.

For example, delays with the issue of loan cheques or fund transfers from the mortgage company might cause a problem for the conveyancing solicitor, who then will have to telephone the mortgage company and wait for a lengthy period on the telephone on hold with little progress! If the solicitor has a good working relationship with the mortgage broker, they might ask that mortgage broker to check into the matter and hurry things along. The mortgage broker is then in a position to contact the mortgage company using a direct broker line (no waiting on hold) and ask them about the delay. Are there any outstanding items to be dealt with and, if so, what are they? This can save two to three days for the buyer at a time when they are waiting to receive the keys. As the mortgage broker is working for the buyer, as is the solicitor, there is no issue with their communication.

The professionals who comprise a buyer's team might be a financial adviser or mortgage broker; a buyer's broker or house-hunter; possibly an architect, an engineer or building surveyor; perhaps a building contractor who has access to the various tradesmen that might be required; and a conveyancing solicitor. Having a good working relationship with all of these property specialists will make the whole transaction more efficient for the buyer and easier to manage. It also should save the buyer money by receiving expert advice, avoiding the classic mistakes and benefiting from the team's suppliers and trade contacts.

Home-buyers cannot afford to sit back and let the purchase happen; they must take responsibility for the investment they are making in their new home. A sensible strategy for buyers is to take the advice of experts, listen to what is being said and then make the decision that is right for them at that particular time.

Inexperienced buyers from the boom years, who find themselves in negative equity and worse, now blame the media, the government and the banks for their situation. The market has blown up since then. Home-buyers who elect to buy at the current time must become fully accountable for their purchase.

Financial Adviser or Mortgage Broker

In the context of property, a financial adviser is professionally trained to work with home-buyers and to guide them through the application process in a manner most likely to achieve mortgage approval at the best possible lending terms and conditions.

They will evaluate the current financial position of the applicant and compare that to where they need to be in order to qualify for a mortgage. Not all applicants will meet the massively elevated criteria of the mortgage companies at the moment. In this scenario, the financial adviser will help the future applicant to put together a financial plan, leading to a successful mortgage application in a longer time frame, possibly three, six or 12 months down the line. The key to a strong and successful working relationship with the financial adviser is finding the right personality for the buyers to deal with and developing trust. Where the financial adviser has been referred to the buyer, this encourages confidence each way.

Many advisers receive a commission from the mortgage company, but these commissions have been greatly reduced in recent years. As a result, some advisers are now charging fees to the buyer in addition to the reduced commission rates. There are also financial advisers whose only source of income is generated from the buyer. There is a perception in the marketplace that only fee-based financial advisers are entirely working for the buyer. This is a generalisation, and perhaps a little unfair; however, buyers are urged to clarify the position regarding fees at the beginning of the relationship and to request a copy of the fee agreement. This is further discussed in Chapter 6, 'Securing Finance'.

Buyer's Broker

A relatively new development in the Irish market, a buyer's broker works exclusively on behalf of the buyers, helping them to define their property search criteria and advising on the local property market. While there is an aspect of house-hunting involved, the principal role of a buyer's broker is to research the particular property, the immediate area and, most importantly, the sellers – all with a view to negotiating a better deal for the buyer. As sellers are usually represented by estate agents, who are professional negotiators, it makes sense for buyers to have access to professional negotiators as well. As buyers' brokers do not sell or list property, and their only fees are generated from the buyer, they are entirely independent in the advice they give.

Estate agents and auctioneers are not included here as they are members of the seller's property team, and buyers need to be aware of this throughout the transaction. Most buyers dread interacting with an estate agent; however, despite bad press, buyers are reminded that there are many professional and reputable firms out there and common courtesy should be maintained. No professional's integrity should be questioned until such time as reason has been given to do so.

Architect

Where buyers are looking for a ready-to-go modern or well-finished home, they may not need the services of an architect; however, for most other buyers, architects can turn almost any building into a prospective home, designed with the buyer in mind. Sometimes seen as a luxury expense by first-time buyers, architects provide other services in addition to good design. For example, they can provide 3D images to buyers who are unsure about the potential of a new home. The sheer volume of very standard, three and four bedroom semi-detached homes mean that buyers in the market rarely come across a house design of note. An architect can alter such a standard space entirely, thus rendering it a unique and stunning home for the buyer at an affordable price. Not only will this result in the buyer acquiring or creating their ideal home, but they are also increasing the value of the home and its chances for subsequent sale. Having a good working relationship with an architect means that buyers can pick up the phone when they have found a house that looks promising and the architect, already familiar with the buyer and his search, will be in a position to talk about the potential of the house. For buyers who struggle to see the design potential of a badly-appointed property, a good architect will be the difference between buying and not buying – they turn layout problems into design opportunities.

Building Surveyor or Engineer

Prior to buying their new home or investment property, every buyer is recommended to engage the services of a structural surveyor to check the property for defects. This is discussed in greater detail in Chapter 17, 'Structural Survey'.

Having an engineer already on board will be a great help to the buyer at the offer stage of the process. Where there are competing bids on a property, the highest price will not necessarily be successful. If the sellers are motivated to sell quickly, they will be looking for the best, immediate unconditional offer. Having telephone access to the surveyor, not to mention some goodwill, the prospective buyer may get the survey carried out the same day in some instances. While the report will take a few days to issue, most surveyors will give a 'thumbs up', or else flag concerns, during the course of the survey, which will enable the buyer to make a decision.

Building Contractor

Builders get a lot of bad press, and certainly not all of it is unwarranted, so buyers in need of a builder are advised to select one based upon a personal recommendation or verifiable references of past clients. Again, having a builder on board at the early stages can be very beneficial to buyers who are actively looking for a 'fixer upper', as the builder might attend a second viewing with the buyer and offer his opinion prior to the buyer engaging a surveyor. A builder also will have a more realistic view of the property and what can be done. Crucially, he will be able to price any work likely to be needed before the buyer commits to buy the property. This will cut down on expenses for the buyer who otherwise might have pursued the property to their financial detriment. The builder's preliminary opinion is in no way a substitute for the structural survey, however.

Solicitor

Good legal advice is essential for buyers but, more importantly, the buyer should engage the services of a solicitor with whom they feel they can work successfully. Good legal advice is of little benefit if the buyer cannot access it when needed. The solicitor, in the course of conveyancing, checks the title to the property and ensures compliance with mortgage, Revenue Commissioners and Property Registration Authority (formerly the Land Registry) formalities. A personal recommendation will be very important here. This is discussed further in Chapter 22, 'The Legal Process'. Buying property tends to bring up other issues too. For example, buyers will be advised to make a will; therefore, a proactive, efficient solicitor that the buyer can communicate with will make the process much more manageable.

The buyer's relationships with each of the team listed above are important and will directly impact on the success of the transaction. Buyers are advised to keep the lines of communication open, to keep the professionals up-to-date and to seek clarification on any issues of concern.

Finally, friends and family who have purchased property in recent years will be in a great position to share experiences, give first-hand advice and refer property services. Buyers are encouraged to listen to it all but, unfortunately, must make the final decisions themselves.

KEY POINTS FROM CHAPTER 4

❖ All property buyers will benefit from access to expert advice and information from professionals working on the ground.

❖ The buyer is advised to put together a personal team of advisers that they are likely to need throughout the transaction – for example, a financial adviser, property buyer's broker, architect, structural engineer, builder and solicitor.

❖ Engage professionals based upon a personal recommendation, verifiable client testimonials or past works carried out.

❖ Engage and create this team very early in the process for maximum benefit. It helps buyers to have access to advice at every step of the way.

❖ Buyers should select the professionals with whom they can work harmoniously. A personality clash with the solicitor will not ease the stress on closing day!

Chapter 5

TAXATION ISSUES

The implications of buying property

Stamp Duty on Residential Property

The first taxation issue that buyers will have to contend with is stamp duty. While this is not called a 'tax', it is in effect a form of taxation or a liability imposed upon the buyer in favour of the Revenue Commissioners in respect of the property purchase.

Reform of the stamp duty regime in Ireland was announced in Budget 2011 and given legislative effect by the *Finance Act 2011*. This reform reduced the rates of stamp duty for all residential properties and all classes of buyers. The current rate of stamp duty payable on residential property in now 1 per cent on properties valued up to €1 million, with 2 per cent applying to properties over €1 million.

All previous reliefs and exemptions from this liability were abolished, which means that first-time buyers are now liable to pay stamp duty on any purchase they make. Previously, residential property transfers under €127,000, and all newly built homes below 125 square metres in size, were exempt for owner occupiers only, that is, not investors. As there is still significant over-supply in the newly built homes market nationwide, this reform may well be considered one or even two years premature.

Under the current legislation, stamp duty must be paid where a parent transfers a residential site to their adult child, irrespective of whether monies have changed hands. This site will be subject to an independent assessment of value.

Mortgage Interest Relief

Rather than a tax liability as above, this is tax relief in respect of interest charged on a mortgage, which is given to the borrower for a period of ~~seven years~~. The home loan must be one that is considered to be a qualifying mortgage, that is to say, it must be a new mortgage for a home; an extension or top-up of an existing home loan that is to be used for the purposes of developing or improving the home; a separate home improvement loan; a re-mortgage or a consolidation of existing qualifying loans, again, used for the purchase, repair or improvement of the home and secured on the deeds of that home. However, switching lenders or mortgage types to achieve better terms and conditions as market forces change is not considered a 'new loan' for the purposes of tax relief. Buyers should be aware that home improvement loans taken out with a different lender to their mortgage company – for example, another bank, building society or the local credit union – also attract this interest relief.

In 2002, the Revenue Commissioners introduced an efficient mechanism for processing this tax benefit whereby the relief is paid at source by the mortgage lender, rather than the borrower having to manually claim the relief at year end. Referred to as tax relief at source (TRS), this provides that the borrower's mortgage account will be credited by the sum equivalent of the tax relief on a monthly basis. Most borrowers do not realise that they do not have to be earning a taxable income to qualify for mortgage interest relief; once the interest is being paid by the borrower, the relief is allowed.

Mortgages taken out from 1 January 2004 to 31 December 2011, subject to the above qualifying criteria, attract mortgage interest relief until 31 December 2017. In fact, as noted earlier, 2011 was to be the final year for home-buyers to avail of the full seven year tax relief on interest. Mortgages taken out from 1 January 2012 to 31 December 2012 will be entitled to mortgage interest relief at ~~25 per cent for first-time buyers~~, and 15 per cent for all other home-buyers. Buyers should note that the relief applies per individual repaying the mortgage and not per mortgage. The phasing out of the TRS scheme will be complete by 31 December 2012 (unless changed again in Budget 2013) and mortgages taken out after that date will not qualify for mortgage interest relief.

Mortgages taken out prior to 1 January 2004 are no longer eligible for mortgage interest relief as the seven-year period has expired; however, top-up loans or equity release loans taken out after 1 January 2004 on these pre-2004 loans may attract mortgage interest relief.

As it can take a period of up to eight weeks for the Revenue Commissioners to process the TRS application and have the lender apply the equivalent credit to the borrower's account, it is advisable to submit a claim for this as soon as the mortgage is in place and repayments commence. Where the borrower submits a claim during the same year in which the mortgage is taken out, the lender will credit the borrower's account with any arrears that may have accrued, but only for that same year period.

Buyers can claim mortgage interest relief until the end of December 2012 by completing the application form online at www.revenue.ie, or obtaining a TRS1P form from their lender or mortgage broker. Where the mortgage is a joint loan, both parties to the loan must complete the form unless they are a married couple.

In the event of difficulties, buyers should speak to their financial advisor, bank or contact the national TRS Helpline on 1890 46 36 26.

Capital Gains Tax

Capital Gains Tax (CGT) is taxation on profit or gains that arise from the sale of capital assets such as land and buildings. Investors should note that the profit from the sale of any interest in property, including a lease, will attract CGT. The tax is actually chargeable upon the disposals of assets, not necessarily the sale.

This means a gift of property will attract CGT if an independent valuation shows a gain or profit from the time of acquisition to the time the property is given. Disposal of the property includes:

- The transfer by sale, exchange, that is, house swap or gift
- The settlement of a real asset on trustees, or
- The receipt of a capital sum derived from real assets such as compensation or insurance money in respect of the loss or destruction of an asset, or for forfeiture or surrender of rights.

Property disposed of in the course of administrating an estate, after the death of the property owner, does not fall within the bounds of CGT. Where such sale or disposal is made, other than to persons connected with the estate, the consideration is deemed to be equal to the market value of the asset at the date of disposal.

All Irish residents, or those persons ordinarily resident within the State for the year of assessment, are liable to pay this tax in respect of chargeable gains accruing in that year upon disposal of the property asset, wherever that asset may be situated. The charge is not just applicable to individuals – it extends to companies, legal trusts and other bodies.

Individuals ordinarily resident, but not necessarily domiciled, in the State are chargeable to tax on gains on the disposal of chargeable assets situated outside Ireland and the United Kingdom, but only to the extent that such gains are remitted to this country. Property owners are advised to seek clarification on their personal status from a qualified taxation advisor.

The computation of the gain to be taxed for CGT purposes looks at the sales proceeds or value of the gift less the cost of the asset and any deductible expenditure, and the appropriate tax rate is then applied. Deductible expenditure was indexed or adjusted for inflation relief for allowable expenses incurred on or before 31 December 2002. It does not apply to allowable expenses incurred on or after 1 January 2003. This indexation adjustment does not apply to such expenses or expenditure incurred within one year of the date of disposal of the asset.

There are many reliefs and exemptions available from CGT and it is important for property owners, and investors in particular, to consider these in advance of devising a strategy for disposal of the property. Notable exemptions are:

1. The first €1,270 of profit or taxable gains by an individual in any given tax year is exempt. For a married couple, this exemption is available to each spouse but is non-transferable.

2. Profits or gains made upon the sale or disposal of a residential property where the house has been used as an individual's only or main residence during that individual's period of ownership.

3. In certain circumstances, any gain arising from the sale or disposal of a property that has been the sole residence of a dependent relative may attract full or partial relief from CGT.

4. A profit or gain on the disposal of a business or farm, through retirement, by an individual aged 55 years or older for a consideration not exceeding €750,000 is exempt from Capital Gains Tax. Where the disposal is made to a child of the individual (or, in certain circumstances, to a nephew or niece), the gain is exempt irrespective of the amount of the consideration.

The current rate of Capital Gains Tax for disposals, including disposals of development land, is 25 per cent and is charged on each tax year running from 1 January to 31 December. A rate of 40 per cent applies to disposals of foreign investment properties. Owners of property overseas are advised to consult the tax code in that country to ensure compliance with all legal obligations.

Capital Gains Tax falls due for payment on one of two possible dates for taxpayers. If the transfer date of the sale or gift giving rise to the chargeable gain arises between 1 January and 30 November, the CGT will be due for payment on 15 December. If the date of transfer is between 1 December and 31

December, the CGT is due for payment on 31 January. Clearly there is a benefit for tax payers in taking a look at the strategic timing of the transfer to take advantage of a CGT payment period of up to 11 months.

There were no changes to Capital Gains Tax rates in Budget 2012; however, in the Government's four year plan, it is intended to increase the scope of CGT charges so property owners will need to watch out for changes from 2013 onwards.

Capital Acquisitions Tax

Capital Acquisitions Tax, as it relates to property, is a tax on any interest in a real asset acquired by way of a gift or inheritance. It incorporates Gift Tax, Inheritance Tax and Discretionary Trust Tax. Gift Tax is charged on taxable gifts acquired on or after 28 February 1974 and Inheritance Tax is charged on taxable inheritances acquired on or after 1 April 1975. A once-off Inheritance Tax applies to property, which is subject to a discretionary trust, on or after 25 January 1984.

CAT is certainly more complex in its calculation than other forms of taxation and, once again, property owners are advised to consult with a qualified taxation specialist to ensure compliance with CAT liabilities.

Valuation of the assets is based on a broad range of issues and the following will need to be considered:

1. The total assets and liabilities of the person or estate making the gift.
2. Whether a will has been made.
3. The number of beneficiaries and their relationship to the giver.
4. Whether business or farm assets are included.
5. Element of personal property.
6. Any savings or investments.
7. Life assurance policies.
8. Possible pension benefits.

Once an assessment of the above has taken place, the taxable value of the entire benefits, gift or inheritance can then be calculated. This is reached by deducting the tax-free group threshold figure, which will vary depending on the relationship between the person making the gift and the beneficiary of the gift or inheritance, from the total amount of the gift or inheritance. Once the total surplus amount is calculated, and the tax liability is combined if there is more than one beneficiary, the Capital Acquisition Tax can be worked out using the current rate of 25 per cent. CAT is then payable on the value of all assets inherited or received by each individual beneficiary.

In order to calculate CAT for new gifts and inheritances received on or after 5 December 2001, consideration will need to be made of all gifts and inheritances received from all sources to an individual beneficiary since 5 December 1991. Rates of tax are adjusted in January of each year to allow for inflation.

Capital Acquisitions Tax-free thresholds were reduced by 20 per cent in Budget 2011. Current group thresholds are shown below.

Group	Relationship to Disponer	Group Threshold
A	Son/daughter	€331,839
B	Parent/brother/sister/niece/nephew/grandchild	€33,185
C	Relationship other than Group A or B	€16,592

Income Tax: For Investors only

Investors must pay tax on received rental income less any deductible expenses. The following is a non-exhaustive list of expenses that may be claimed by the investor landlord:

1. Interest on borrowed money used in the purchase, improvement or repair of the property.

2. Mortgage protection policy costs.

3. Repairs and general upkeep of the property – note that investors may not claim the cost of their own time or labour.

4. Ground rents – rent *payable by* the landlord.

5. Service charges – for example, water rates or refuse collection – not discharged directly by the tenant.

6. Cost of utilities – for example, gas, electricity, telephone line rental – paid after default by a tenant or previous tenant.

7. Insurance of the property.

8. Management of the letting, where a letting agent is engaged.

9. Legal expenses associated with the letting.

10. Accountancy fees arising from preparation of the rental income tax return.

It is important to note that pre-letting expenses are not allowable tax deductions, with the exception of professional fees (legal and auctioneering) incurred in the first letting. Capital allowances may be allowed on items bought to furnish the property and are deducted from income for tax purposes. This is referred to as a claim for 'wear and tear', and the allowable rate is currently 12.5 per cent per year over an eight year period.

Section 23 Properties

Over the past decade, Irish investors have relied heavily on tax incentive properties, and in particular Section 23 properties, to balance their portfolios. Major changes to these incentive schemes were announced in Budget 2011, but due to intensive lobbying of government by many bodies within the industry, not to mention a question of constitutionality, these changes were not given legislative effect in the *Finance Act 2011*. The likely consequences for investors are discussed later in greater detail in Chapter 20.

Rent a Room Scheme

Many home-buyers plan to supplement their income and mitigate the expenses associated with the purchase of a property by renting out a room for a year or two. Under the current scheme, buyers can rent out the spare room(s) to generate up to €10,000 rental income per year tax-free. This income is not subject to the income levy introduced in 2010. The rules of the scheme are quite strict in that there can be no additional charges for extras, so the agreed rent must include all facilities provided, such as laundry, heat, electricity, internet access and/or cable television. The income earned through this scheme has no impact on the homeowner's tax liability on selling on their home (Capital Acquisitions Tax) and, most interestingly, it will not affect any entitlements to social welfare. Any person intending to avail of this scheme is statutorily obliged to file an annual tax return prior to finding a tenant.

As renting a room is relatively informal, homeowners are advised to use a rent book (available for approximately €2 in most stationery shops nationwide) to record the value and payment of rent, notice period and any conditions of renting. While the rent a room scheme was left untouched in Budgets 2011 and 2012, participants should watch for changes in forthcoming budgets as the government seek to abolish reliefs.

Non-Principal Private Residence (NPPR)

A tax on non-principal private residences was introduced in 2009 at a current rate of €200 *per annum*, irrespective of the size, or value, of the property. Payment is due on or before 31 May and any late payments will incur a penalty in the sum of €20 per month until such time as the liability has been discharged. Significantly, this is not a tax on second homes but rather on any residential property that is not currently occupied by the owner. Therefore, struggling homeowners who have relocated temporarily in search of work, or to take up a temporary contract outside commuting distance of their home, will be hit with this tax. This tax is being collected by local authorities nationwide in the hope of redeeming their much depleted balance sheets after a historic drop in commercial rates collection. This is not perceived to be an equitable tax by homeowners, and it remains to be seen whether the government will review this initiative in 2012 when a residential property tax is likely to be introduced.

Residential Property Tax

Some level of property taxation was expected to be introduced in Budget 2012 and there was much relief among homeowners and prospective buyers alike when no such charge was put in place. In the long term, the tax seems likely to be one based on a combination of building size and site value. In fact, one of the many reasons why the government chose not to introduce such a measure at this time is the inherent difficulty in ascertaining 'market value' of any given property or site in the current market. All indications are that homes in a position of verifiable negative equity, and those uninhabited houses more prevalent in rural areas, will be granted some form of exemption. At the present time, this is merely speculation. For property owners in 2012, there is no property tax; however, homeowners and buyers should prepare for some level of taxation from 2013 onwards.

Household Charge

In Budget 2012, the government introduced an interim measure called the household charge. This is a form of property taxation, which applies at a rate of €100 on each residential property within the State. Despite the name, the charge applies only to the property owners, with limited exemptions. It was envisaged that this charge would apply each year for a period of two years, to allow the government time to create a national database that would facilitate a fairer site value tax.

However, in reality, the household charge has been poorly received by the Irish people and, at the time of writing, less than half of the estimated 1.6 million households liable have paid.

There is speculation that the charge may be scrapped altogether; however, it is more likely that non-payment will go unenforced in 2012. It is certainly expected that the government will introduce a new property tax, similar to most other European countries, sooner than expected, in Budget 2013. The National Property Price Register is due to be fully operational by summer 2012; if this happens, a site value tax would be possible by early 2013.

KEY POINTS FROM CHAPTER 5

❖ The stamp duty regime was reformed in Budget 2011. Rates are now 1 per cent for properties valued below €1 million and 2 per cent for properties in excess of this value.

❖ Other tax liabilities may include Capital Acquisitions Tax (CAT) and Capital Gains Tax (CGT).

❖ Existing tax reliefs, most notably Section 23 and Section 50, are being phased out.

❖ 2011 was the final year for buyers to obtain full mortgage interest payment relief under the TRS scheme. Buyers in 2012 will receive a reduced payment.

❖ Investors and non-owner/occupiers are subject to an annual Non-Principal Private Residence Tax (NPPR) of €200 for each property.

Chapter 6

SECURING FINANCE

Contributed by well-known market commentator and QFA
Karl Deeter, *operations manager of Irish Mortgage*
*Brokers (*www.mortgagebrokers.ie*)*

Estimates for 2011 put total mortgage lending in the region of €2.3 to €2.4bn, this is a drop of almost 95 per cent from peak lending in 2006. In terms of the number of loans, the last time we saw so few draw-downs was exactly 40 years ago in 1971. That was a year that came on the heels of the longest-lasting bank strike in Irish history, from May to November of 1970. Given that lenders are actively telling the market that they both can, and will, lend in 2012 gives us the belief that the low point in mortgage credit has now passed.

How much above €2.4bn in lending remains to be seen. The Government is doing what it can to bring people into the market. Tax relief at source has been continued for another year, and the National Asset Management Agency (NAMA) has plans to sell close to 1,000 properties with a 'negative equity insurance' built into the purchase.

But, if we have hit rock bottom, it does not mean that credit will now be free and easy. Far from it, banks have returned to more prudent underwriting and margins have increased; trackers are long gone and fixed rates are unavailable or priced in a manner that is intended to stop buyers from opting for one. For the near future, it will be a standard variable rate world.

For the majority of people who buy a home using a mortgage, it is the single biggest financial decision they ever make. A mortgage is effectively the second of two sales: the first is when you sign the contract for the property and the 'purchase' occurs; the second is when you then sell that property to the bank in return for the money (the mortgage). In return, the bank has the 'first lien' or first right to the proceeds of any consequent sale until such time as the loan is cleared in its entirety.

Ability to Repay

The main thing a lender wants is assurance that they will be repaid, and that the person has the capacity and desire to repay in full. This is difficult to assess. Let me put you in the shoes of an underwriter (the person who sanctions the loan) for a moment ...

A file arrives on your desk. In it are copies of ID, address verification, bank statements, a salary certificate and a few other documents. From those, and those alone, you must decide whether to lend a person you have never met amounts of up to €350,000 or €400,000 (above these amounts, the decision usually goes to a higher level of management called the 'credit committee').

This may seem like little to go on but, in the right hands, a set of bank statements gives good insight into a person. I'll give a brief example.

Joe Bloggs has large cash withdrawals on Friday and Saturday nights, his Laser card is used in nightclubs (the names show up on the statement), and he is living at home. He says he saves but that he gives the money to his mother to 'mind' for him as it avoids the temptation of spending. He has a good permanent job, earning €50,000 a year, but at the end of every month he is slightly over-drawn. And as for paying rent? He gives his mother €100 a week.

I cannot tell you how common this profile or one similar to it is, and as you may suspect already, Joe is unmortgagable. The first thing he would be told upon contacting our brokerage is to get his affairs in order, at least to the point where a lender can read into them better – so the savings must be to an account in his own name; ~~if he is paying rent, then do it by standing order~~; and, for the love of God, stop going into overdraft every month (this is referred to as 'hardcore' overdraft – where the person effectively has a loan out because they are in the red every month).

Then we have Jane Bloggs, Joe's sister. She saves in the local Credit Union and never goes into overdraft. She moved out of home a few years ago and rents an apartment with her boyfriend, who is also applying for a loan with her. They pay rent *via* standing order and they have a 10 per cent deposit which they built up themselves. She earns less than her brother (€40,000) and her job is also permanent.

The profile here could not be more different. For a start, ~~two people on an application gives the lender far greater security as they are liable 'jointly and severable'~~ (together or each on their own) for the loan. All their financial affairs are easy to track and understand for the underwriter – who again, does not know either of them – and questions regarding money usage are easily determined. This is the kind of case that is likely to go ahead because ability to repay is already proven.

Ability to repay is demonstrated when you pay a rent that is equal to or above the monthly cost of the loan you are hoping to take out. Throw in savings and the vista looks even better. Sometimes, people think that renting is viewed as 'bad' by a lender. Far from it, it demonstrates experience of making monthly payments and living on your own; the obvious downside is that it is hard to save and rent at the same time.

When you want to get a home, we advise people to get an ~~approval in principle (AIP) first~~. You do not *have* to do this, but it does make life easier if you are looking at property that you stand a chance of actually affording.

Every lender has their own calculator for determining how much they will lend: some of them use a multiple of salary, others use a 'net income' calculation and more use a similar 'debt service ratio' (DSR) calculation.

Depending on circumstances, there may be large disparities between one lender and the next, but all calculations are the same in that they are a decision-making tool for the bank, which tends not to go outside of their set criteria (which was once pretty common).

Deposits

The typical deposit required is at least 10 per cent (although AIB accepts 8 per cent deposits for first-time buyers), and some lenders look for 20 per cent. The remainder of the money for the property that you borrow is the mortgage and, when expressed as a percentage, it is called the 'loan to value' (LTV) – we love using acronyms in finance!

The way to calculate the LTV is to divide the loan amount by the property value and express the result as a percentage; it even works on properties in negative equity. If you want €80,000 towards a property costing €100,000, then it is an 80 per cent LTV proposition. If you owed €100,000 on a property valued at €80,000, then your LTV is 125 per cent and therefore you are 25 per cent in negative equity. The calculation works both ways.

A growing trend in lending is that of 'tiered variable rates'. These are standard variable rates that get more expensive as your LTV increases. One trend in 2012 is for the gap in pricing to widen; by that I mean that, instead of there being a difference of 0.5 per cent between loans at 80 per cent and 90 per cent LTV, the difference will be more like 1 per cent. Pricing for greater risk will become more common.

One thing worth mentioning if you are a PAYE worker is that doing a tax return can help towards a deposit. You can register for 'PAYE Anytime' on the Revenue website (**www.revenue.ie**). You can go back four years and get a refund if you paid for education, refuse, rent (s473, *Taxes Consolidation Act*), and medical or dental bills. There is a comprehensive list on the site – just search for 'IT1'. The Revenue will send you a P21 Balancing Statement. We regularly see refunds in excess of €4,000, making this something you should not skip over! You can get an accountant or a tax refund company to do this for you.

Bank *versus* Broker

My vested interest in brokerage is obvious, but I would not stay in the intermediary space unless I truly believed in it. In the past, using a broker helped because the market was more complex, and some banks (such as Bank of Scotland) only distributed through brokers (as KBC effectively still does now). Now, with more restricted choice and availability, a broker tends to be of benefit in dealing with banks that have more stringent criteria and ask far more questions than they used to – effectively, a broker does much of the running around so you do not have to.

An independent broker must have at least five lending agencies – something you should clarify before dealing with a broker – and that means you do not have to walk around five or more banks with your application; it all can be done in one spot. A good mortgage broker also will know how to 'package' a case so that it gives the underwriter the easiest interpretation of the proposal – something branch staff often are not as good at because they focus on many areas at once, not just lending.

The downside is that sometimes there are fees involved, which banks do not usually charge – but if a fee is going to be raised, it must be clearly pointed out in the 'terms of business' letter that a broker is legally obliged to present prior to giving advice.

How do you pick a broker? Referral is a good option. You can look on the Internet. Or you can call one of the broker associations like the Professional Insurance Brokers Association or find a broker on its website (**www.piba.ie**).

When you meet a broker for the first time, ask the person about their level of experience, how many years they have been brokering, how many agencies they represent, what qualifications they hold and any other questions you might have. Anybody worth their salt will be more than happy to tell you about their record and achievements!

Being Ready (or Not)

At least two in five of the people we talk to do not stand a chance of getting a loan when they first express an interest in buying a home. For that reason, we quite often send them off with some simple advice on how to get their affairs in order so that they do stand a chance in six or 12 months' time.

This often means saving more, making their financial situation easier to understand and reducing outgoings as well as clearing existing loans.

Sometimes people are upset at this news, but it is merely a reflection of the lending environment and any advisor doing their job right will not want to put a person through the application process in vain.

Banks that are Lending

As of writing, several banks are for all intents 'closed for business', including National Irish Bank, Ulster Bank, and Haven Mortgages (a subsidiary of EBS). There are a few who are half-heartedly lending (permanent tsb, EBS, ICS – a subsidiary of Bank of Ireland). And then there are the banks that are open for business – but that does not mean they are lending freely – namely, KBC, AIB and Bank of Ireland. This may change through the year but I suspect that, of the three lending now, only AIB and Bank of Ireland will be in the same space in 2012.

Other considerations are the amount that you want to borrow and where the property is based. When it comes to one bedroom apartments, for instance, AIB and ICS/BOI will lend to a maximum of 75 per cent LTV, EBS will go to a maximum of 65 per cent and some lenders simply do not want to bank them at all. There are other curiosities in the market as well, such as KBC's maximum loan being dependent on the population in the area; recently, they were lending 90 per cent for areas with a population of more than 15,000 people and 80 per cent below that!

Lending is a strange place of late - and that is likely to remain the case through 2012/2013.

The Irish Credit Bureau

Bad credit will be rampant in years to come, especially since we start the year with over 110,000 mortgages in some kind of trouble, about 68,000 in actual arrears of some sort, while a further 70,000 have had to seek some kind of restructuring (generally to 'interest only'). The next year will be a time of huge change because banks will have to draw a line under the loans that will be worked with and those that are 'unsustainable'.

For those who are not in trouble, the Irish Credit Bureau (ICB) keeps track of payment histories for the various types of credit people have – mortgages, credit cards, car loans, credit union loans, etc. If you are at all worried about your own credit history, then it is best to get a copy (which you are legally entitled to under the *Data Protection Acts, 1988 & 2003*) at a cost of €6. Just go to **www.icb.ie**, where you can do it online.

Unless you have, or had, a credit problem, the ICB check will not really be a factor in your application other than signing to authorise the lender to carry out a search. If there is a problem though, and you do not believe it is fair or correct, then you will need to find out what it is and get it sorted. Once or twice a year, we encounter this – sometimes, it is as simple as a person having a date of birth, address, or name similar to another person and the information gets mixed up. But it is best to remove some such potential difficulties before you apply for a mortgage.

The Process ...

You will likely deal with several people in buying a property, including:

- A broker or banker
- A buyer's broker/agent
- An insurance broker or company
- A solicitor, and
- Depending on the property, a surveyor or architect.

The approach we take at Irish Mortgage Brokers is to consult with the potential buyer, either in a meeting or over the phone. From this conversation, we determine the best course of action, which generally involves a requirement to gather documentation.

The documentation a lender typically looks for is:

- Proof of identification – passport, driver's licence
- Proof of address – utility bill or bank statement less than three months old.

The first two are to satisfy Anti-money Laundering and Prevention of Terrorism legislation and are referred to as the 'KYC docs' (KYC stands for 'Know Your Client') – they establish who you are.

Next are documents that establish financial facts about you.

If you are employed, you will be asked for:

- A salary certificate to be completed and stamped by your employer
- Last year's P60 (sometimes a December payslip also works)
- 6 months of consecutive payslips
- 6 months of most recent current account bank statements
- Savings statements
- Credit card statements
- Other loan statements
- Any other documentation that may be deemed relevant, including marriage licences, evidence of legal matters (if separated/divorced, the agreement connected to this may be required or if you are living in Ireland on a visa).

If you are self-employed or a company director, you will be asked for:

- Three years of signed accounts for your business or company

- A tax balancing statement or tax statement from your accountant
- Details of business bank accounts for the last year
- 6 months of the most recent current account statements
- From time to time, there are other company-specific matters that are required; be aware that banks will check CRO status and may make other company search-related enquiries as well.

In the background, irrespective of employment status, you will undergo an ICB search and the person handling your application also will complete the calculators we mentioned earlier.

With any luck, this will result in an approval in principle (AIP), which is not worth the paper it is written on, though it does give an initial indication of borrowing capacity and it lists any further documentation or criteria that will apply.

The reason I say an AIP is not much good is that it is an indication rather than a commitment by the lender and if criteria or rates change, they affect people with an AIP whereas people with actual loan offers will have a certain period of time to close the loan before (for instance) the rates go up.

The other side of the transaction is the property itself and, to negotiate this process, you will be dealing with the estate agent who instructs contracts to be sent to your solicitor. You also will need several insurances (covered in Chapter 7, 'Protecting the Purchase'), and the actual 'deal' is done is *via* your solicitor.

So when you see a property you actually want, and it is within the amount on your AIP, you then make an offer. If it is accepted, the estate agent will instruct the vendor (seller) to issue contracts to your solicitor.

You normally have 21 days to sign these – although with various issues, it can take a longer or shorter period. During that time, you must get your financial affairs in order. That means instructing a valuation – this is done *via* the mortgage broker or the bank – which gives value details about the property to the lender so they can judge the quality of the security for the loan (remember as we mentioned earlier, the bank is going to buy this house too!).

In some circumstances, usually with older properties, the lender also may require a structural survey or an architect's report. In a newly-built property, they will want to see that the property is fully completed and 'snagged' – the person who does a snaglist is often a surveyor (as opposed to an architect or valuer, but that is not a set rule).

The valuation and any other documentation required in the AIP must go to the lender. You also may need to obtain life cover at this point – as it is often a requirement in the loan contract to have it – so make sure you do not delay in getting applications filled in, in particular if you have any known health issues. Failure to obtain life cover can scupper deals – and does so regularly.

The lender now will put together a 'loan offer pack', which has a letter of offer and several other assignments enclosed – this all goes to your solicitor. From this point onwards, your solicitor will be your main point of contact. They will complete the conveyance, which is the transfer of a property from one person to another, along with registering the encumbrance of the mortgage, which will establish the 'lien' mentioned earlier.

This process never goes smoothly. Once you are aware of that, and accept it, it takes out most of the stress. Because you are liaising with up to six different parties, the process can be hard to navigate, and lines of responsibility are often blurred.

The best defence is to have a good team in your corner. For that reason, I personally think it is worth testing your team prior to going with them – for instance, call the solicitor's office, see if somebody answers the phone or if it is a voice messaging service. In fact, it is worth doing this with anybody you are going to be dealing with – including your mortgage broker, if you use one. It may seem silly but ease of contact is really important in the run-up to a closing.

Self-build

Some of you may be building a home on a plot. This is more common outside of cities and, with it, comes a plethora of other issue to consider. If you are building a home, banks will normally want to know that an architect or engineer is standing over the job and that they will issue certificates of compliance (with building regulations) at the end.

Before draw-down, you may have site acquisition costs (if you are getting a site from a family member at a minimum value, you will need to prove ownership *via* the Property Registration Authority (formerly, the Land Registry) and you may be asked for 'stamping' evidence (that taxes were paid on transfer).

Banks will lend you to purchase a site and then build a house but that would be a chapter unto its own so, if you are in that situation, enlist a good team – I know I keep repeating that but it cannot be stressed enough. On a self-build, depending on your building experience, you may be reduced to only being good for picking up the tab – and that is when the team matter most.

To proceed, you will need build costs and evidence of planning. The build cost in a fixed price contract is as per the tendering process done by your architect. Evidence of planning comes from your local authority – and do not forget to factor in the costs of contributions, which go up depending on the services you connect to (there is generally one price for the general contribution, with additional costs if you connect to water and more if you connect to sewage as well).

ESB connection is also a consideration, as is your distance from the nearest line. This does not matter so much in cities but, in rural areas, it can become a large overhead.

From experience, I have found a fixed price contract to be the best choice and, when competitively quoted for, not much more expensive than direct labour, which will take away from you in lost time what it makes up in savings. If you happen to be a trades-person, then I would advise self-building for sure but, if you are not, no amount of DIY experience or a year spent as an apprentice can make up for it.

Everybody who has self-builds that go pear-shaped have two things in common in our experience – they think they know what they are doing when they are actually clueless and they hammer sub-contractors on price but do not realise that the 'very competitive' quote is missing vital elements of the jobs, which then arise as 'extras'.

Even when you look at a standard Royal Institute of Architects of Ireland (RIAI) contract, an inexperienced eye may miss that things like 'internal doors' and door frames/hanging of same may not be included. A halfway decent internal door costs €100; the ironmongery can be another €40 or more; the cost of handles depend on your taste, then a finishing carpenter on day rate and it all adds up to a big cost you did not see coming.

That is why you hear about people 'going over' on budget. You can bring any project in on budget as long as you do not have some great unforeseen (like finding an underground river while doing your groundworks). Everybody may say 'building always goes over budget' – I'm telling you it doesn't. Nine times in 10, the client makes it go over *via* changes and additional works. Builders, of course, are more than happy to do extras; it's the 'cream on top' of a job. A growing trend is to quote at break-even just to keep the company turning over and, in those cases, extras may be the only source of the builder's profit.

Despite the stories that hit the headlines, the standard of builder in Ireland is quite good. Before enlisting one, go talk to people they did work for, ask them what they had done, how much it cost, what kind of problems they had and how they were solved.

Then ask the builder to show a job that didn't go so well. That might seem downright cheeky. It is – in fact, it is meant to be. Before you part with many tens of thousands of euro, it is worth getting an insight into the personality of the person you will be dealing with for several months of your life. Like any walk of life, construction is full of different personality types. You will need to both trust and get along with your builder but keep a healthy dose of scepticism as well – especially during the second fix! Talk to somebody who has built a house and perhaps they can explain it better to you, but suffice to say everybody who self-builds learns a lot ... usually the hard way!

Types of Mortgages

Mortgages can be either fixed or not, so by definition there are broadly two types with various sub-categories.

Fixed rate mortgages represent about 125,000 mortgage accounts as of early 2012. They are not very popular and some banks are either not lending on a fixed basis or they are 'pricing the rate out' so that it is so penal that nobody takes them up on it. This has to do with bank funding because they will usually create an interest rate swap with a counterparty and, due to Irish banks being out of favour, the counter-party will only take this on at a high rate (which translates into a high price for the purchaser of a fixed rate mortgage).

The terms you can fix for are generally one, two, three, five and 10 year terms – although some banks have odd terms like six and seven-year fixed rates too.

Fixed rates are beneficial because they give a set outgoing per month. By and large, fixed rate borrowers pay a premium for their rate. In that respect, it is like a 'rate insurance'; you pay a certain premium for the knowledge that there is no scope for a rate increase for the duration that you fix for. The downside is that rates can move in your favour and, because the rate is fixed, you do not benefit from the lower rates. There was a glut of fixed rates taken up in 2007. Many of those buyers regret the decision because it was made at a time of rising rates and rates have been on a downward trend (except for two rate hikes in 2011) since mid-2008. If you want out of a fixed rate – even to sell the property – you face a penalty called a 'break fee', which relates to the cost of exiting the fixed rate. In this instance, the lender will tell you the fee and how it is calculated.

Variable rates come in different guises. There are the famous 'tracker mortgages' that track the European Central Bank (ECB) interest rate by a fixed margin above it. The best of these was National Irish Bank's 0.5 per cent tracker, meaning that, at a 1 per cent base rate, the mortgage rate was a mere 1.5 per cent! The majority of tracker mortgages were in the region of 1% above ECB. There are about 400,000 such accounts and they are a thorn in the lenders' side. They are doing all they can to get rid of them; some have even taken to offering bonuses for paying off your mortgage early if you have one!

The reason is that trackers are a loss-maker even when you repay them. If a bank is being charged 3 per cent or more to borrow but they have lent out the money on a tracker mortgage at 2 per cent, it requires no great mathematical ability to realise that in time bad things will happen. Think of an everyday example: Jane opens a bread shop, she buys loaves of bread for €2 and sells them for €1 – Jane's business plan needs serious revision. Trackers are no longer available and will not be again for the foreseeable future.

The other type of variable rate is a standard variable rate (SVR), which has since morphed into a tiered variable rate (TVR). The standard variable comes with no price promise like trackers have. In fact, a large point of contention in the last two years was that banks kept hitting their SVR customers with rate hikes in an effort to balance out the losses they were making on trackers.

Standard variables are slowly giving way to the new breed of TVRs, which is a standard variable rate but with pricing partly LTV-dependent. So below 50 per cent LTV, you will get a great rate; from 50 per cent to 80 per cent, you get a decent price; but above 80 per cent, you are paying the most as this is the more risky end of lending.

The ECB is likely to bring the base rate to a historic low this year. This may mean that we see low rates along, with a small increase in lending and reduced property prices, so the ingredients for a good long term purchase are there; but there is no guarantee that the buyer of 2012 will not regret that decision just as buyers in previous years have.

Other Sources of Funding

There are a few other options out there as well.

Home Choice Loan

This is a State-run lending agency, which will probably close soon because they have a team of people working there and have done fewer mortgages in three years than our firm does in a fortnight. The idea at inception was to fill the void left by banks that were not lending and to give a financing opportunity similar to a traditional mortgage *via* the Housing Finance Agency. The scheme has had virtually no uptake and is a well-intentioned failure. I do not think it will be here this time next year.

Shared Ownership

This is a purchase that buys (at a minimum) 40 per cent of the property, while the remainder (60 per cent) is rented from the local authority. So it is partly a loan and partly rent – which is charged at 4.3 per cent of the unpurchased part (so it is almost *like* a mortgage rate payment in cost terms).

To try for shared ownership, you have to go on the list at your local authority and seek approval to be part of the scheme. That means being eligible under the criteria, which means you earn less than €40,000 a year. On a joint application, it is different: you multiply the higher income by 2.5 and then add on the lower income and the total must be less than €100,000. For example: Person 1 earns €23,000 and Person 2 earns €18,000 – thus, 23 x 2.5 = 57.5 + 18 = €58,500. So, in this instance, the couple would qualify for a shared ownership application.

If your household income in the last income tax year was less than €28,000, you will qualify for a rent subsidy that varies from €1,050 to €2,550 *per annum*, once the subsidy does not reduce the rent to less than €1 per week.

Council buyouts

Sometimes, people see this as a separate classification. Personally, I describe it as a being a renter (local authority tenant) who buys the property from their landlord (local authority). Often this is done at a discount to the buyer, in lieu of years spent in the property. Only a few banks deal with this type of purchase, so you will need advice if you want to do this. Local authorities are now authorised, once certain conditions are met, to sell blocks of flats to the occupants, so this may be an increasingly popular trend in the future.

What Else to Watch Out for ...

Make sure that your solicitor holds money back if there are any conditions to be met upon completion and that the seller is aware of this. We have recommended this many times only to see it not happen and then the buyer wants to know what they should do because the seller took a fridge and washing machine they were meant to leave behind.

Front-side negotiation is Carol's forte. I just want to say that, if you do make any agreement, it is best to formalise it by asking that it is put into the contract by your solicitor. Solicitors may say this is not necessary. I am telling you from my years of experience that all that does is give many solicitors more work to do post-purchase that never should have occurred.

The only other odd thing we have seen is a delay on the seller in moving out. That is why you should ask if you are getting vacant possession or if the seller is being given a certain amount of time to move out – I do not advise agreeing to the latter.

A Final Note on Problems with Mortgages ...

No matter how complex your mortgage application may be, it is still the easy part of being a home-owner. The hard part is making the payments every single month, irrespective of your health, luck, or employment status.

There are huge problems in bank loan books at present. As many as 20 per cent of mortgages are thought to have some level of 'stress' in them – where they are either greater than one month in arrears or have been moved to paying only the interest as a brand of forbearance ('not enforcing a contract in return for some kind of action on behalf of the other party' – in practice, that means the bank does not repossess your home as long as you make your interest payments, for example).

There will be big changes in debt law as required by the Troika bailout and the good news is that banks no longer hold all of the cards. There is a new *Code of Conduct on Mortgage Arrears* and a new *Consumer Protection Code* that must be obeyed by financial institutions. If you get into trouble on a mortgage, you have far more protection in 2012 than you ever did before and banks must deal fairly and sympathetically with people who are struggling to pay. The key is to 'engage' and that means returning calls and letters. If you think you may be 'headed' towards arrears, call the bank, ask to be treated as a 'pre-arrears' case and start early on a solution.

Chapter 7

PROTECTING YOUR PURCHASE

Necessary insurances and life assurance

When a property purchase is financed by way of a mortgage in Ireland, there is a mandatory level of insurance required in order to secure the bank's interest in the property. This is not optional. Buyers will have no choice as to whether or not they seek cover. The decision buyers will face is the extent of additional insurance cover they desire in order to better protect their individual interest in the home. This additional insurance is to give homeowners some level of protection, over and above that afforded to the mortgage provider, and will come at a higher cost to buyers.

The mandatory insurance is generally a mortgage protection policy and home insurance, which takes into consideration the building and contents. In the course of arranging the mortgage, most lenders generally will use the opportunity to up-sell a range of insurance and life assurance products to borrowers. Please be aware that borrowers are absolutely not obliged to buy any insurance or assurance product from their mortgage lender. At this stage, those borrowers are best advised to shop around, or have their mortgage broker shop around, for the most suitable products at the best possible price.

Mortgage Protection

Mortgage protection insurance is one of the two mandatory policies required by Irish lenders. It is essentially a life assurance policy that covers the extent of borrowings and ensures that a borrower's liability to the mortgage company is repaid in the event of their death or that of their spouse.

There is a wide range of available options in the Irish market. The most basic policy type provides for cover over the term of the mortgage on a decreasing premium, so that in the event of death, the outstanding mortgage will be cleared. A higher degree of cover is available on what is commonly referred to as a level basis, which provides for a specified sum to be paid in the event of death. The cost of this latter policy type is higher, but the benefit is much greater as the sum paid out will cover the outstanding debt mortgage with a surplus cash balance going to the borrower's dependents. Buyers must keep in mind that cover only extends for the term or duration of the mortgage and should not confuse it with full life assurance.

Serious Illness

This is an optional add-on to the required mortgage protection policy and one that has increased in popularity over the past decade. It provides for the repayment of the outstanding mortgage, or part thereof, in the event that the borrower suffers from a serious, life-threatening illness. The policy document will list the illnesses considered to be 'life-threatening' for this purpose, and buyers are advised to review the list of covered illnesses very carefully before making any decision. It is an additional cost to the borrower, but one that affords genuine peace of mind for many property buyers.

Payment Protection Insurance

Payment protection insurance (PPI) covers the borrower's repayments on the mortgage if they suffer from loss of income due to an accident, illness or redundancy. It is important to note that the repayments will be covered for a specified period, usually 12 months, and will only come into effect after one month of lost income.

This is a more expensive type of policy for borrowers, and most brokers would encourage such borrowers to look into permanent health insurance (PHI) as a more comprehensive, cost-efficient alternative in certain circumstances. It is not a mandatory policy but one that many single income families in particular will find conducive to their home and working life situation.

Home Insurance

Home insurance is the second of two mandatory policies for buyers who financed their property by way of a mortgage. As the property is likely to be the most valuable material possession for most people, it is certainly advisable to insure it against fire, theft and other damage regardless of whether it is financed by way of a mortgage.

The home insurance, encompassing building and contents insurance, is usually but not necessarily sold as a single policy that includes:

1. Buildings insurance, which covers damage to the building.

2. Contents insurance, which covers any loss of or damage to the contents within the home.

3. All-risks protection, which covers loss of or damage to listed valuables, even when outside the home.

4. Liability insurance, which covers injury to other people in or around the home.

Combining buildings and contents cover into one policy usually represents the best value for buyers. There is a large selection of home insurance policies on the market to choose from, with considerable differences between them. Buyers are encouraged to read the terms and conditions to find out comprehensively what is included. They should always seek clarification where terms appear unclear.

As a general rule, the smaller the print, the more important the term is. When faced with competing insurance or life assurance policies, it is important to remember that the policy offering the lowest premium generally offers the least protection.

Buildings Insurance

Buildings insurance generally covers the immovable features of the property. Usually these are specified as the structure of the home, such as the roof, walls, windows and doors, together with permanent fittings and fixtures, including tile and flooring and all kitchen and bathroom fittings. In most policies, outbuildings such as a garden shed, garage or workshop building are covered, as are garden walls, gates and fences.

Of equal importance is a provision for temporary alternative housing if the property is destroyed or rendered uninhabitable. This allows the homeowner to move out or rent another home while the damage is being repaired without incurring addition expense.

Causes of Damage Generally Covered	Causes of Damage Not Generally Covered
• Fire, explosion, lightning, or earthquake • Flooding and storm – building only • Subsidence (restrictions apply) • Riot, vandalism, or other violent acts • Burglary or attempted burglary that results in damage to the property, fixtures or fittings • Water or oil escaping from a services appliance i.e. burst pipes • Vehicles or animals damaging buildings, walls, gates or fences • Falling trees and branches.	• Storms affecting gates and fences • Flooding or subsidence where this is a usual occurrence in the area and was undisclosed by the buyers • Acts of terrorism • Standard wear and tear in the structure or the inside of the property • Failure of the homeowners to maintain property • Negligent tradesman – this must be claimed from their own public liability insurance.

The table above shows a non-exhaustive list of the events generally covered, and those excluded, under the standard terms and conditions of most policies. As mentioned, these may vary from one insurance company to another.

Homeowners should make themselves aware of the policy excess, as they will not be in a position to make a claim for any amount that is less than the agreed excess on the policy. Buildings insurance is not based on the market value but rather the reinstatement value – in other words, the amount of money it would take to rebuild the property. The best source of up-to-date building costs in Ireland is the Society of Chartered Surveyors.

Knowing the reinstatement value of the property is very important for buyers, as the value provided to the insurance company dictates the premium to be paid and the likely sum paid out in the event of a claim. Under-insurance may result in a payout that is not sufficient to fully repair or rebuild the property if it is damaged. Over-insurance will not necessarily result in a larger payout or any extra benefit, but will certainly drive up the premium for the property owner. This is because the insurance company will only ever pay out the actual cost of rebuilding.

Contents Insurance
This type of policy provides insurance cover for the movable objects in the property. As mentioned, it may be taken out as a separate policy from buildings insurance or combined with it for cost-efficiency. A separate contents insurance policy is suitable for those occupants of a property who do not own it.

As with a buildings insurance policy, the onus is very much on the homeowner to insure the contents for the correct amount. This is generally the actual cost of replacement. For many items, this can be difficult to assess so buyers must carry out some research to ensure that they would be in a position to replace any items lost or damaged in the future. There is usually a limit on the value that can be claimed for any individual item, so it is sensible to list certain valuable items, such as antiques, separately within the policy document.

Events and Contents Generally Covered	**Events and Contents Not Generally Covered**
• Accidental loss of or damage to listed items • Accidental damage to household equipment i.e. TV or stereo • Loss of or damage to items moved from the property temporarily – for example, when moving home • Food spoils resulting from power failure or the fridge or freezer breaking down • Cash stolen from the property home, up to a certain limit.	• Loss or damage arising if the property is unoccupied for a period of 30 days (varies) • Money or valuables stolen from the property if not properly secured • Title deeds, bonds, bills of exchange, promissory notes (contract of money), cheques, stamps, valuable documents of any kind, manuscripts, medals and coins • Motor vehicles and accessories (separate policy) • Standard wear and tear or resulting damage.

All-risks Cover

This is another optional extra offered by insurers in the course of brokering any standard home insurance policy. It provides additional protection to the homeowner against loss, theft or accidental damage to personal valuables such as jewellery. The nature of this cover is to ensure that special items, which the homeowner might take on trips, are covered inside and outside the home, both in Ireland and overseas. There will generally be some restriction to the overseas cover – for example, 60 days on any single trip. The benefit of all-risks cover for the homeowner is that, in the event of a successful claim being processed, the insurer will either have to pay out the cash value of the item or pay to have same repaired or replaced.

The homeowner may opt for an overall value for unspecified items without having to list each one; however, with this type of policy an upper limit generally applies to the value that each unspecified item may be claimed for. This means that the insurer would only pay that fixed maximum amount for any specific article stolen or damage, irrespective of value.

Liability Insurance

Liability insurance is generally included in any standard home insurance policy and provides cover in the event that someone visiting the home, or working within the home, suffers an illness or injures themselves in an accident for which the homeowner is found to have been at fault. Add-ons to this type of policy might extend to damage caused by the homeowner outside the home – for example, where accidental damage is caused to another and/or the property of another as a direct result of the insured homeowner doing or failing to do something. In such an event, the policy would cover the costs, medical expenses and possibly legal fees that the homeowner would ordinarily be liable for. There will be a limit imposed on the extent of cover available.

Title Insurance

This insurance deals with the legal title to property, rather than the property itself. Unlike other forms of insurance that insure against things that may happen in the future, title insurance protects against matters that happened in the past. This kind of policy is not particularly common in Ireland since its introduction in 1998, and to date it has been used exclusively for re-mortgages rather than purchase of property. It protects the homeowner from any loss resulting from title defects, fraud or forgery related to title of the property. If appropriate, this is taken out with the advice of a solicitor and is covered later in this handbook under Chapter 22, 'The Legal Process'.

Some Points of Note for Homeowners When Shopping Around for Insurance

- There are restrictions and exclusions in every insurance policy; most are standard, but some may vary from one insurance company to another. It is imperative that homeowners read through the policy document thoroughly and satisfy themselves that they understand its entirety.

- Most policies will contain an excess – this is simply the amount that the insured will need to pay themselves before the insurance kicks in. This also means that where the sum sought is less than the agreed excess figure, no claim can be made.

- Most insurers will increase the value of the buildings and contents cover automatically when they issue the annual renewal notice. This is done to keep long-term insured assets sufficiently covered as their value increases in line with inflation. Also referred to as indexation, this measure ensures that buildings are not under-insured. However, in the current market, where the cost of building has decreased significantly, it is worthwhile for homeowners to check the amount of cover to avoid being over-insured.

Key Points from Chapter 7

- ❖ Mandatory insurances (if property is financed by way of a mortgage) include mortgage protection and home insurance, which may comprise building, contents and liability insurance.

- ❖ Optional (but often recommended) insurances include payment protection insurance, serious illness cover and all-risks insurance.

Chapter 8

FINDING THE RIGHT PROPERTY

Sources of publicly-marketed property

The over-supply of houses and apartments in Ireland has dominated most property commentary since 2007. Vacancy levels have reached somewhere between 230,000 and 280,000 units, double the number that would be considered normal in a functioning property market. This figure does not include second-hand homes that are currently being offered for sale by the existing owner. With such an over-supply in the market, it seems incredible that buyers are having difficulty finding their ideal home or property investment, but that is exactly what is happening. The statistical data reporting is distorting the local market in many areas; for example, over-supply might be high in a particular area of re-generation, but these might be made up of apartments or poorly appointed townhouses. In reality, few semi-detached houses might be available. In this type of scenario, the issue is not necessarily over-supply or low levels of demand, but rather a mismatch of the two. This is seen in the vicinity of Dublin city where buyers have demand for houses but the majority of available stock is apartments. It also can be seen all around the country, and is a problem best attributed to the planning decisions of local authorities over the past decade.

Leaving aside the desirability of one type of housing over another, the sheer volume of stock is making the task of wading through property listings to find a quality home akin to finding a proverbial needle in a haystack. In addition to the high stocks of available properties, there are now many different sources for properties that must be investigated. The number of sources is ever-increasing as anxious sellers compete for a small pool of ready buyers. With so many online and offline sources of marketed properties, buyers may find it difficult to monitor each one. Also, it is important for house-hunters to remember that not all *available* properties are marketed publicly or offered for sale on the open market. Off-market property sourcing is covered in Chapter 9, 'Sourcing Off-Market Opportunities'. The main sources of advertised or marketed properties for sale are listed below; buyers are advised that this list is non-exhaustive as sellers and their agents are becoming more creative to deal with increased competition from other sellers/properties to attract buyers.

Online Resources

The Internet has changed the way that house-hunters find property but, if used in isolation, prospective home-buyers will lose out on many opportunities. Every estate agency group or franchise, and most individual estate agents, will have their own dedicated website. Where the search is concentrated locally or over quite a small area, buyers are advised to start here as properties may be listed in so many different sites on the Internet that it is possible to miss a few, but properties always appear on the estate agents' own website.

The most commonly used resources are dedicated property sales websites, but there are many other property portals online, including those listed below.

Property Sales Websites
- www.daft.ie
- www.globrix.ie
- www.myhome.ie

- www.property.ie
- www.propertypromoters.ie

Private Seller Websites
- www.4salebyowner.ie
- www.easydeals.ie
- www.privateseller.ie
- www.sellityourself.ie

Other Online Sources
- www.add.ie
- www.adoos.ie
- www.buyandsell.ie
- www.citylocal.ie
- www.ebay.ie

These websites can be a great resource for time-poor buyers, if used correctly. But they can vary in terms of quality and substance; that is to say, while they are efficient, they are not always the most effective way to find the right property. Buyers should watch out for a couple of classic techniques that sellers and their agents, and indeed the websites themselves, use to manipulate buyers. For example:

- The pricing is unreliable in that it is likely to be either optimistic or strategic. Where the seller is unrealistic, and ignores the advice of his estate agent (who must act in accordance with his client's instructions), the advertised price may not reflect market realities. This is harmful for buyers who use this information to assess local values. Strategic pricing can be high or low, depending upon the strategy employed. Strategically low prices are used to entice more buyers to the property, thereby increasing competition and, as a result, raising the bids on a particular property. Strategically high prices are less common. An example of this was seen in 2009 when two apartments in a very small, established and desirable development came on the market at the same time with a price difference in excess of €130,000. On investigation, the seller of the less expensive apartment was in a chain, having already secured a new home and needed to sell straight away. The seller of the higher-priced apartment turned out not to be a seller at all, but rather a concerned homeowner who felt that her home was being devalued by the actions of her neighbour (which, arguably, it was). Her listing was merely an individual attempt to maintain value, or perceived value, in the development. In reality, the true market value was somewhere between the two listed prices. This raises the side issue of data integrity when compiling industry reports.

- Buyers should also watch out for duplication, or several listings for the same property. Many times, this is the innocent result of the seller engaging more than one estate agent; however, it is increasingly common to find up to three listings for a particular property, each with a slightly different address and guide price. This is done to take advantage of proximity to neighbouring areas that are considered more desirable and therefore more valuable. Even sellers who have already engaged the services of an estate agent are starting to list their own properties on these websites at slightly lower prices – effectively competing with their own property through the estate agent.

- There is an underhand practice starting to seep into the market by a minority of property salespeople (generally not auctioneers or accredited estate agencies), struggling to make a commission, which involves the inappropriate use of the established practice of open agency. (Open agency is commonly and appropriately used in the sale and letting of commercial property, whereby the owner of the property lets a large number of estate agencies know that the property is available and any firm is free to introduce buyers – similar to the international multiple listings system.) This is modelled on an American approach but does not translate well to the Irish residential market as there is a different system of selling here, which does not include multiple listings. This practice is being distorted by salespeople advertising a particular property or development and purporting to have the authority of the seller, which in fact they do not. As a result, the buyer is being misled on the entire offering. In the course of pre-negotiations (covered in Chapter 11), this is stamped out as buyers are advised to ensure that the selling agent has authority from the owner to sell the property. An example of this was seen in the Dublin market in mid-2010, when a buyer, having seen the property online, contacted the salesperson to ask questions and to arrange a viewing. The lack of authority was uncovered when the viewings were not authorised by the owner. Incidentally, the guide price, which clearly was a *guess*timate, was out by more than 15 per cent.

- It should be noted that the chat forums, feedback and comments on some of these websites are often heavily and sometimes unfairly moderated to promote a single premise: 'we are property, property is good'.

- The final issue for buyers to note is false claims by websites purporting to have every property on the market and that buyers need look no further. Genuinely, buyers should take note that this is nonsense – it is simply not true and they should absolutely look further.

There are many offline sources of property in Ireland, and while some will seem primitive or even archaic to first-time buyers who have only considered online sources, they can be of equal, if not greater, importance when looking for a home. The added advantage offline is that the buyer can gain a more complete picture of the local market. The market in a single town in County Kildare, for example, will be of little relevance to a buyer in the north of County Clare. Similarly, the market in north County Dublin will be of little relevance to a buyer in the south of the county.

The most obvious way to find available property offline is for the buyer to visit the area and its immediate surroundings, spend some time noting the *For Sale* signs (in particular, note which estate agency has the most signs up and the most marked 'sale agreed') and speak to local shop-owners or people in the vicinity.

This will give the buyers a clear indication of the dominant estate agents in the area, and these agents, in turn, will become a primary route to property. Buyers are advised to drop into these offices if they are in the area to talk to local agents. Buyers may also consult with local property buyers' brokers or house-hunters. While these professionals do not list or sell property, they will be in a position to find suitable properties, generally at discounted prices, for a fee. This type of service will be of most benefit to inexperienced buyers or buyers who do not know the local area well.

Some private sellers advertise in the classified section of the local or national papers so it might be worthwhile for buyers to keep an eye on this. Generally, the phrasing of the advertisement will tell a lot about the sellers, that is, how motivated they are to sell. Most national and some local newspapers have a regular property feature or supplement. These tend to be good sources for information as well as for lists of properties. Buyers can keep up to date on developments that are scheduled to come on stream and read the results of any auctions that have taken place. The current national publications are shown below.

Publication	Available
Daily Mail, Property feature	Wednesdays
Irish Independent, Property supplement	Fridays
Sunday Business Post, Property supplement	Sundays
The Irish Times, Property supplement	Thursdays
The Sunday Times (Irish edition), Home magazine	Sundays

KEY POINTS FROM CHAPTER 8

❖ Online sources of publicly-marketed property include:

  o Property portals or websites

  o Estate agents' websites

  o Other property-related sites and forums/chat

  o General advertising websites that host a property section.

❖ Offline resources include:

  o Estate agents' windows

  o 'For Sale' signs

  o Newspapers property supplements

  o Classified ads.

Chapter 9

SOURCING OFF-MARKET OPPORTUNITIES

Finding that hidden gem

Long-time house-hunters will probably have experienced the sight of new owners moving into a local area that they have been watching diligently for months or even years, and saying to themselves, 'How did we miss that opportunity?' The short answer is that, in actual fact, the opportunity was never afforded to them. It is most likely that the property in question was sold quietly, off-market, that is, away from the open market. This will confirm what most people will have long suspected: that not all properties available for sale are offered to the general public on the open market. While this type of transaction is common among investors of both commercial and residential property, home-buyers in the past rarely got the chance to compete; however, with a bit of hard work and shoe leather, this could change. There is no reliable data to deduce what proportion of properties are accessed off-market, however anecdotal evidence within the industry indicates that the figure could be as high as 30 per cent.

Buyers immediately tend to feel uneasy about this – they feel it reaffirms stereotypical market criticisms of underhandedness. In practical terms, this genuinely is not the case. The seller is under no obligation to market the property in the same way that a body like NAMA is. It is not unethical or suspect; there are any number of reasons why a seller may opt for a quiet or off-market sale, namely:

- The seller specifically may require privacy.
- The seller may be in financial distress and need to sell quickly.
- In the event of marital breakdown, the court may order the sale of the property and the owners, to avoid further distress to the family, may opt for a quiet sale.
- A property owner may receive a direct approach from a buyer and consider selling even though he had not planned to do so.
- An investment property may be sold quietly to avoid disruption of the tenancy. The tenant, of course, would be notified of the transfer of ownership.
- The property might have some complications that would not suit all buyers so the seller actually targeted a few potential buyers directly.
- Probate properties tend to pass quietly due to the long lead-in time, that is, buyers are aware that the property is vacant and may make direct approaches to the executor or beneficiaries.
- The seller may be changing jobs, relocating for work or emigrating and does not want others to know until the property is sold.

Buyers should not treat the off-market search as being separate or independent to their other house-hunting activities. All sources of property, both on- and off-market, ought to be pursued at the same time. This requires a bit of time and hard work on the part of the buyer, but it should greatly increase the likelihood of finding the ideal property.

Sources of Off-market Properties

As the sources of off-market property are many and varied, the list below should not be considered exhaustive by any means. It is merely to demonstrate known and currently used sources. The main thing for buyers is get into the habit of talking to people they meet, let people know that they are in the market for a new home or investment property. The biggest mistake that buyers can make when house-hunting is to limit themselves – be creative!

Take the phenomenal rise in social media as an example: just imagine if a buyer was to send a tweet (a very short message, similar to an SMS text message, through the Twitter network) that they are looking for a property in a specific area immediately. What would the likely response be? Who knows, but for the sake of typing 140 characters, it seems worth a try! The key to a successful house-hunt is variety.

Buyers should not discriminate about who they speak to. Property has always been a popular topic of conversation, and buyers can learn a lot by listening. Ireland is a very small country and local knowledge is worth as much as any property report. When buyers are visiting their chosen areas, they should make an effort to talk to residents and ask questions about the neighbourhood, any local developments planned and whatever else they can think off. This might offer some leads to the buyers or point them in the right direction.

Examples of off-market sources include:

- Where a buyer identifies a particular area of interest, but cannot find a suitable house on the open market, it is worth driving around the area to identify vacant or boarded up properties that are likely to be sold. It is recommended that house-hunters then make direct approaches to homeowners by knocking on doors, or by searching property ownership details through the Property Registration Authority, and writing to the registered owner at the address and to the solicitor's office (this will appear on the PRA search).

- Another source of property might be previously marketed houses that were subsequently withdrawn from the market, or properties that failed to sell at auction over the past few years but are still vacant. Such properties might be available and the reason they are not on the open market is because the homeowner has decided to wait until the market picks up, which is entirely reasonable in the current climate. The lesson here is to seek clarification from the owner directly or through the previous estate agent who is most likely still in contact with them. Never assume that because a property is withdrawn from the open market that it is no longer available; there are many forces at work and buyers should always follow up if interested. The same process should be applied to residential sites or properties where planning permission has been refused; a frustrated owner may be happy to offload at a good price to a buyer who is buying it as it stands, that is, not based on future potential to extend.

- Many frustrated homeowners, who are desperate to move but cannot off-load their existing home, are looking to property swaps as a viable option in the current market. Websites dedicated to this have become more prevalent in the past two years, when homeowners thought that this might be an alternative to staying in a property under threat of negative equity, which it is not. The reality is that the homeowners are not stuck with their home – they are stuck with their mortgage and that mortgage is secured on the home so the owner, essentially, has no asset to swap. In terms of financing, a swap would mean discharging the existing mortgage and taking on a new one in respect of the newly-swapped property. There are a number of problems here, most notably that the bank is not going to accept a lesser or inferior form of security. Also, the homeowner may not qualify for a mortgage at this time of restricted credit and tighter lending requirements. This does not stop the owner from trying. Every property forum at the moment has enquiries from people looking to swap. So, what does this mean for house-hunters?

Essentially, every property offered *via* house swap is available to buy off-market. Buyers should keep an eye on these websites and forums and contact the owners about any suitable properties.

- In Chapter 4, the concept of the buyer's property team was discussed. This is a great place for buyers to start. They should discuss their search criteria with each professional and see if they have any information or knowledge of upcoming sales. In terms of follow-up, it is important to check in regularly with each member of the property team to ensure that any opportunities that arise are sent the buyer's way.

- Estate agents are a rich source of off-market information and properties for a number of reasons. Firstly, they have detailed knowledge of their specific area or 'patch'. Secondly, they carry out valuations independently for banks and other lending institutions so they know when an agreed property sale subsequently falls through, even if it was previously listed by another agency. The third reason is also the most important, and refers to the valuations that are requested by homeowners themselves. This private valuation may be may needed in the course of a financial review, or where the joint owners are separating and must deal with the property. However, a private valuation is most commonly requested in advance of the homeowners placing the property on the market. Tip for buyers: December is probably the best month for sourcing off-market properties through an estate agent as any prospective sellers will usually hold off until the New Year because of the expected low interest of buyers during the holidays. Buyers who make themselves available and seek out property at this time may well be granted access to the property. If it is suitable, there is time to strike a good deal with little or no competition from other buyers.

- Local authorities nationwide are sitting on a stock of vacant and sometimes unfinished properties (or finished properties in unfinished developments) that they will need to off-load in the future. Preliminary searches will reveal all of the properties and it is up to the buyer to identify potentially suitable areas or properties before approaching the council. Investors traditionally had this market covered so buyers will need to be astute in selecting properties and have some idea of their values. Methods of valuation are discussed in Chapter 13.

- Other professionals like accountants, family solicitors, probate solicitors and insolvency practitioners are well placed to pass on opportunities, but they will only do so if the buyers are known to them and some level of goodwill exists. Buyers are advised to start with their own personal property team and move on from there.

- In addition to the sources listed above, buyers are generally urged to pay attention and engage with the world around them. Buyers should be following news stories; for example, if a receiver is appointed to a development company, five minutes' research will give a list of that company's development sites.

- The most common example of routine off-market sales in practice are where an estate agent is given a portfolio of properties belonging to the same investor, investment company or bank, with instructions to sell but not at the same time so that the market does not become flooded with below market value properties. What happens here is that perhaps two properties are released on the open market and the others are promoted quietly to potentially interested buyers. In time, if they are not sold, these properties may hit the open market, but this could take many months. The most likely outcome is that the off-market properties will be secured before the time comes and they will never appear on the open market. The first a buyer will know about this process is when the owner or tenant moves in to occupy the property.

Off-market Property Sourcing – A Case Study

The prospective home-buyers in this instance were a young couple, first-time buyers. Peter was a financial consultant with an office in Dublin 2, but he serviced the Dublin city and county area and travelled for work appointments. Marcella was office-based and worked in the Blanchardstown area. Neither was originally from Dublin and rented in the Dublin 15 area. In terms of location to buy, both Peter and Marcella wanted to remain close to their rented home as they had lived there for several years (in the same house) and had a good relationship with the neighbours. The development in which they currently rented was ideal, but having only approximately 40 homes, houses did not come on the open market regularly. After waiting for approximately a year, Peter and Marcella decided in late 2010 that it was the right time in terms of both their careers, their savings and the limited opportunity to avail of the TRS scheme for them to enter the property market. As their chosen area was not yielding results on the open market, they decided to take some direct action, so, with some professional assistance, they decided to directly target their current and a neighbouring development.

The first step they took was to approach their existing landlord about the possibility of a sale; however, he was not inclined to sell at that time. The next step they took was to draft a letter outlining their circumstances and search requirements and deliver it to each home in the two identified developments. They got several responses but became disheartened when the owners placed an inflated value on their respective homes. After meeting several homeowners who were considering selling, they sought independent valuations of each of the potentially suitable homes and were in a position to negotiate with another couple with a young family who had outgrown their three bedroom home. Peter and Marcella placed a bid of 15 per cent under the independent valuation, which was rejected outright, but an agreement was finally reached at 10 per cent below the stated valuation on the basis of saved estate agency and marketing fees.

The booking deposit was paid directly to the vendor's solicitor (always advisable in a private sale) and the conveyancing process began. Peter and Marcella thus secured a home in their ideal location by putting in a bit of thought and effort. Significantly, a good relationship had built up between the buyers and sellers that resulted in quality furnishings being left at no extra charge, and the vendors were allowed additional time to move as the closing was postponed for almost three months to accommodate the local primary school term ending.

The vendors were able to move forward with their plans for a larger home, safe in the knowledge that their existing home was sold — and Peter and Marcella got their ideal home at a good price.

KEY POINTS FROM CHAPTER 9

❖ There are many reasons for off-market sales, for example:
- o Financial distress
- o Marital breakdown
- o Privacy concerns
- o Strategic – not wanting to flood the market
- o Where buyer makes a direct approach.

❖ Sources of off-market property can be anyone the buyer comes in contact with, but most likely are one of the following:
- o Insolvency practitioner

- o Probate solicitor
- o Family law solicitor
- o Accountant or financial adviser
- o Banks.

❖ Off-market purchases tend to be below market value, as the buyer is rewarded for a quick decision to buy and an early closing.

Chapter 10

SITE SELECTION

Finding a suitable site for self-building

There are many reasons why prospective home-owners would consider building their own home, not least because of the design freedom it affords or the end result of a home that suits the needs of the entire family. It also can be a more cost-efficient way to acquiring the home of their dreams. There are a few architecturally stunning homes on the market at the moment, with asking prices slashed in line with market trends; however, these properties are in the minority and still outside the budget range of many buyers. The current stock of available property is overwhelmingly apartments, townhouses and semi-detached units that were built in the last decade. These properties are generally perceived to be of a poorer quality and lacking in design.

For buyers who are committed to building and creating their own ideal home, there are a number of issues to be worked through and steps to be taken. The first steps will be those outlined in earlier chapters of this handbook:

1. Deciding if this is the right time to be building a home.
2. Assembling a property team, which is crucial for self-build homes. An architect should be engaged early in the process and usually will get involved in the planning stage, so it is important for the buyers to find a professional with whom they can work harmoniously.

3. Securing finance at an early stage is definitely advised, as not all lenders are willing to consider this type of project in the current market, particularly with access to credit so restricted.

4. Finding the right site upon which to build the dream home.

The Site

Building a new home is exciting, but it can be stressful if the buyer is experiencing difficulties finding the perfect site, which is really the most important decision to be made. Most other decisions throughout the building will be dictated to some degree by local authority planning terms and conditions, budgetary restrictions or practical realities. Knowing what to look for in a potential site can save the buyer time, expense and frustration.

As a general rule of design, the site comes first and the home plan evolves from the surrounding plot and landscape. Of course, in Ireland, most rural, one-off, newly-built homes are on family land, that is, the site is or was part of the family farm or lands, so this is the most common position from which to start. While the design of the home will not be done until a site has been secured, it will be necessary for the buyer to have some idea about the size or particular features of the intended home, as this will help determine the features or particular aspects needed in the site. It is worthwhile consulting with the architect on this prior to looking for sites, as most architects will have experience in helping inexperienced home builders to define their needs and what they want from the property. This information will be useful when it comes time for sourcing the site and comparing it with available alternatives.

Prospective self-builders who do not have access to land and are looking to acquire a site will find very few offered on the open market. This, in large part, is due to the restrictive approach to planning in rural areas. The approach to rural planning is best described as negative with exceptions, rather than positive in certain instances. Because of this, land-owners and estate agents realise that there is no point offering for sale a site that is subject to planning, if planning can only be granted to certain family members or local qualifying applicants.

The option then facing the prospective buyer is whether to acquire a site with planning permission already in place. The advantage of this is that the buyer knows with certainty that a property can be built there. The disadvantages are the price, which will be up to 50 per cent more expensive than a site that is sold subject to planning permission; the location, which the buyer will have little choice in, as there are very few available (on- or off-market) sites with full planning permission; and, most importantly, buyers also are acquiring the home design that the existing land-owner got approved by the local authority. Usually this can be altered slightly or changes may be allowed, but these changes will be relatively minor in nature and subject to further approval.

Buyers might consider acquiring what is commonly referred to as a serviced site. This means that gas, sewage and electricity lines, as well as possible phone lines and other services, will already be in place. Usually these serviced sites are small, with a choice of two or three house types, and they are often accompanied with a contract to build the house. In effect, the buyer is not building their home but rather having an above average input to the development of the property. The end result will be similar to a small, private housing estate. For people who are committed to creating their unique home on a private, self-contained plot, serviced sites are rarely a viable option.

The most popular option for buyers who wish to build their own home is to find an affordable greenfield site, in a suitably convenient location, and apply for planning permission to build a new home that has been designed especially for them and their family.

Finding a Site

The steps involved are:

- The first thing buyers must do is pinpoint an area or a number of areas where they would like to build, having regard to local schools, facilities and commuting distance to work.

- The next step is to see what sites are available to buy. This can be done by using the various on- and off-market sources of property listed in Chapters 8 and 9. The most effective source of residential sites is the local estate agent or property buyers' broker, who will know of local land-owners who might be interested in selling a site. These agents/brokers are usually well-versed in local authority planning guidelines for the immediate area. Ordnance Survey (**www.osi.ie**) maps are a worthwhile investment for buyers.

- Buyers are advised to make contact with the local city or county council and to get a copy of the *Local Area Plan*, which each local authority produces. These plans are drawn up for seven years and chart the planned development in the area over this seven-year period. It will help buyers to better understand zoning and how it might affect them. This can be done online but a trip to the local office will be far more worthwhile for buyers as they can ask questions and seek clarification on issues.

- In addition to the search carried out through the estate agent, buyers should drive around the area of interest and try to identify potential sites. One opportunity here will be where agricultural land with road frontage already has been interrupted by one or two houses (which most likely qualified for exemptions from planning restrictions), the local authority generally will permit its development as an 'infill site'. Property ownership details in Ireland are a matter of public record and the buyer can obtain full names, addresses and solicitor contact details through the Property Registration Authority. Direct approaches may be made by the buyer to the land-owner; however, in rural areas, buyers generally will find it more effective to have this done through the local estate agent. In other words, the buyer can raise an interest in the land, and the estate agent will approach the seller who, if interested, will engage the estate agent to conduct the sale. Buyers may proceed themselves or seek representation, but it is important to be clear on the estate agent's role, which is to represent the local land-owner.

- Buyers are advised to bring their architect to view the site prior to agreeing to the purchase. There are a number of reasons for this: first, the architect is working exclusively for the buyer so will give a reasoned opinion of the site and the likelihood of achieving planning permission; secondly, architects are experienced in the likely pitfalls of certain sites and will be in a great position to offer points of note or of caution; thirdly, and most importantly, the architect knows what the buyer is hoping to achieve by purchasing the land and will be able to advise on the design implications of the site.

Tips for Viewing One-off Residential Sites

1. Look at neighbouring buildings:
   - Are there any signs of damage; if so, what is the cause?
   - Is the ground sloping? What could be the effects of that?
   - If there are any gaps between buildings, there may be some reason why building could not take place in that location.
2. What is the place name? Could it mean something?
   - For example, River View would suggest proximity to a river.

3. Talk to local people about previous uses:

   - For example, if the site was previously used as a dump or as a bog, it would indicate artificially-filled or marshy ground.

4. Walk the site and immediately adjoining land and keep an eye out for the following:

   - Type of ground – surface condition

   - Any open trenches

   - Vegetation – certain plants indicate marshy ground

   - Evidence of previous use of site – might it have been a filled site, watch for contamination

   - Local rivers or streams – possibilities of flooding, check groundwater levels after heavy rain.

Planning Applications in Brief

Buyers should note that the information below is not intended as advice on specific issues relating to each individual planning application, and buyers should discuss their application with their architect or a qualified engineer.

By engaging the architect at such an early stage, buyers effectively can ease themselves into the planning process by focusing only on sites that offer a reasonable prospect of achieving full planning permission. As referred to previously, all planning is (or should be) based upon the *Local Area Plan* or *Local Development Plan* for any particular area. These six- to seven-year plans generally are available to view on-line and also at the local planning office. All site buyers should familiarise themselves with the plan for their area of interest and surrounding areas. In addition to the *Local Area Plan*, it is important for buyers to know what factors the local planners will be taking into account when assessing their application for planning permission. For instance, buyers will need to consider what effect the house will have on the environment as it is an area that planners will be looking at in detail before any permission is granted. Also, planners will consider how the structure will fit with the existing landscape. Planners will want to know what services options are available in terms of water, electricity and sewage. Buyers are well-advised, when looking at waste management, to choose the system that would cause the least damage to the local environment.

Buyers should be aware of the main types of planning permission that they are likely to come across: outline planning permission and full planning permission. Outline planning permission is essentially permission in principle. Buyers use it to ascertain whether the planning authority agrees in principle to them building a house on any particular site. For this type of application, the buyer need only submit the plans and particulars that are necessary to enable the planning authority to make a decision in relation to the site, layout or other proposals for development. The buyers usually will have a period of three years in which to submit full and details designs to achieve full planning permission (referred to as permission consequent) before commencing work. Full planning permission is most commonly sought by buyers who have all plans and designs in place and are in a position to proceed with the construction work. The term of this permission is usually four to five years.

Buyers should note with caution that it is an offence to carry out any work that requires planning permission without first having the necessary permission in place. Possible consequences are a fine, imprisonment and eventual demolition of the property. It is possible, in limited circumstances, to apply for retention, that is, planning permission to retain an unauthorised development, but buyers are urged to seek professional advice if such an issue arises.

Application forms may be downloaded from the local authority website or collected from any of the local authority offices. Upon completion, these forms, together with the required documentation and fees, should be returned to the planning department of the relevant authority. Below is a non-exhaustive list of the most commonly required documentation:

1. Application form fully completed and signed.

2. 6" Ordnance Survey map, scale 1:10560, indicating location of the site.

3. 25" Ordnance Survey map, scale 1:2500, with site boundaries outlined in red. Adjacent land in applicant's control must be outlined in blue and wayleaves in yellow.

4. Site layout plan, scale 1:500, with the site outlined in red, with the north point showing, also showing the levels or contours where applicable. The position of the site notice affixed to the land or structure must also be shown on the site layout plan or on a separate original map.

5. Detailed structural drawings, specifications, etc. of the proposed development. These drawings should be clearly scaled and dimensioned, and must be in metric scale of not less than 1:200.

6. Schedule listing the plans, drawings and maps described in 2-5 above.

7. Public notices: The original page of a newspaper containing the notice and five copies, plus six copies of a white site notice. If the application refers to a site for which a valid application was submitted within the last six months, the site notice must be yellow.

8. Site suitability report, completed on the local authority's form, detailing trial hole and percolation test results carried out within the last 12 months by a suitably qualified person holding adequate professional indemnity insurance.

9. Treatment plant specification.

Six copies of the application and all supporting documentation must be submitted, together with the appropriate application fee. In relation to the paperwork, all maps must be original Ordnance

Survey maps carrying a red stamp, or stamped with a license number from the Ordnance Survey Office, and the north point should be clearly indicated.

The application then is assessed by the local authority and placed on the planning register in the planning authority offices for public inspection. Any member of the public has the right to inspect or purchase a copy of the planning permission and, upon payment of a fee of €20, may make a written submission or observation on it within five weeks of the date of receipt of the planning application. After considering all information, and referring to the *Local Development Plan*, a decision will be made by the planners and communicated to the buyer in writing.

In the event of planning permission being denied, a reason must be given to the applicant. The buyer then has a period of four weeks from the decision date to appeal to An Bord Pleanála.

KEY POINTS FROM CHAPTER 10

❖ Self-building is still the most cost-efficient way for buyers to acquire the home of their dreams, as the cost of building reduced in line with the costs of buying.

❖ Architecturally-designed homes do not really figure in the stock of available properties, as the over-supply tends to be made up of apartments and poorly-designed three bedroom semi-detached houses.

❖ Buyers should secure a site first, then move on to the design stage. Bring the architect to view the site.

❖ Get to know the local authority as they will become the buyer's new best friend when it comes to finding a rural site.

❖ Obtain a copy of the *Local Development Plan* for the area.

Chapter 11

PRE-NEGOTIATION

The key to finding motivated sellers

This is the first of three chapters in this handbook dedicated to the practicalities of property negotiating. The reason it is broken down into three chapters is because property buyers will find it necessary to use this natural skill at three distinct stages throughout the buying process. Each stage will require a very different type of research, approach and strategy. It is not complicated – time-consuming, but not complicated. In fact, the very idea behind breaking down the negotiations in this way is a direct response to typical human behaviour and how we react in certain circumstances. By acting in a more logical and natural way, the buyer's approach should appeal to the logical and natural senses of the seller and/or their agent to ensure a greater level of co-operation. The principal advantage for the buyer is that they do not have to memorise a set of so-called rules that feel unnatural or underhand. The first step is for buyers to get rid of any dated preconceptions and mental blocks that they might be holding on to. Property negotiation does not have to be feared – it is simply a part of the process of buying a home. Like all processes, it requires input from the buyer and some level of focus to achieve positive results.

Prospective home-buyers tend to have certain perceptions of the property market – unfortunately, mainly negative ones. They are invariably put off by so-called 'tricks of the trade'. Tricks, by their very nature, are fleeting illusions. They are not real; therefore any results from trickery are unlikely to be of any lasting, material benefit. The good news is that, with a bit of hard work and shoe leather, buyers can ensure a more successful outcome by following the strategies outlined throughout this handbook.

Many people consider property negotiation to be a minefield. Traditionally, 'negotiation' took place over a series of tense conversations after the opening offer was made. In too many instances, it was that part of the buying process where the relationship between estate agent and buyer broke down, with any goodwill previously earned lost. Estate agents are the epitome of all that is wrong with the market, according to buyers. While they continue to get a lot of bad press, the reality is that most estate agents are honest professionals just trying to do their job. They may seem uncooperative and occasionally tardy when it comes to viewings, but most buyers, for their part, also manage the relationship very badly by offering little respect or fair play to estate agents. This mutual antagonism comes from a lack of understanding of the estate agents' role in the buying and selling of property. Simply put, the estate agent has no role in buying. Their sole objective is to represent the interests of their client, the seller, by achieving the highest possible sale price. Their only obligation to the buyer is to answer any specific questions relating to the property truthfully.

Understanding this single point will help the buyer enormously, as they can then make an informed decision whether to go it alone or to have their interests represented professionally by an independent buyers' broker or agency. In 2006, the property market was still buoyant and there was a lot of competition for good value homes so negotiations were tough. For buyers, it was no longer sufficient to out-manoeuvre or out-negotiate the estate agent on individual cases as it was proving to be too much of a 'hit and miss' approach. Also, bargains were tough to find because of a lack of information. More effective ways to find motivated sellers had to be created. The old way of negotiating on price *after* the buyer had shown an interest, usually by viewing and making a subsequent offer, did not work. To be fair, it probably worked better for the seller, but it did not work at all for the buyer. It was then the concept of pre-negotiation was introduced by property buyers' brokers.

The practice of property pre-negotiation is undoubtedly easier for a professional to undertake. However, confident buyers who are diligent in their research and who do not mind hearing the word "No" will find the challenge financially rewarding. To explain it best, estate agents may be described as having a dual aspect to their role – they wear two hats, so to speak. Firstly, they wear their sales hat to market the property in question. While in sales mode, they attract buyers to view the property and, at that viewing, they present the property in its most favourable light, all the while hoping that the buyer will fall in love with the property. As soon as that happens, the estate agent knows that the sales phase has been successful and moves smoothly (some more smoothly than others) into the next phase. Once an offer is made, the sales hat the smiling estate agent was wearing comes off, only to be replaced with a professional negotiator's hat. The buyer, disarmed by the change, is in a vulnerable position. The estate agent at this stage knows that the buyer wants to secure this property – worse than that, he knows their plans for the third bedroom and where they are planning to knock that kitchen wall to allow for an open dining experience! Any advantage that the buyer may have held is gone. Traditionally, this is where the primitive dance of negotiation begins.

So how does the buyer know if he has overstepped the boundaries during the viewings? The simplest test is that if they have viewed their favourite house so many times that the auctioneer is invited to their wedding, there is little point in negotiating hard – they have already lost. If they love the house, by all means they can go ahead and buy it, but they should not be surprised when they find that they are facing a 'genuine bottom price' that mirrors the original asking price of three months ago.

The good news for property buyers is that a simple change of behaviour at the start of the entire process can flip this on its head and give buyers back the advantage. What the buyer can do is simply reverse the traditional, or expected, approach by negotiating with the estate agent while he is still in sales mode. This is done by compiling a list of potentially suitable properties, aiming high and not being put off by an excessively high guide price. Buyers should include properties that are marketed up to 50 per cent in excess of their budgets. For example, if tasked with sourcing a property worth €500,000, include properties up to €700,000 or maybe €750,000 in the current market. The list of potential properties could be anywhere from 50 to over 200. Buyers are best advised to narrow down their first choices to approximately 40 or 50 properties. They generally will see an overlap of sellers – for instance, some estate agents might have 12 properties from their list whereas others may only have one or two. It is worth rating the properties with each agent in order of preference – that is, start at the best or most suitable ones and work backwards where necessary.

The next step is for the buyer or the property buyers' broker to contact the owner, if it is a direct sale, or the estate agency to discuss their interest in the properties. They should make it clear that they are interested in the properties specifically short-listed. It is advisable to start with one particular property, and ask whether the owners would be interested in selling the property at the buyer's predefined budget, say €500,000. As the property is currently at a guide price of €700,000, the likely initial response will be 'No way!'. However, if the buyer lets the estate agent know that they are genuine buyers, have finance ready and are serious about the property, at least they will get some information. Buyers will likely be told that there is a mortgage on the property and the seller cannot sell for that price, which is useful information as the buyers now know that the property is genuinely outside of their budget and they can move on to the next one. Or the agent will tell them that €500,000 will not secure the property, but he may give the buyer an indication of how much will be required.

The other response they might get is that the agent tries to arrange a viewing. This is a very positive outcome for the buyer at this stage. If it happens, it is likely because the estate agent knows that the owner can sell at this price. Buyers should not agree to view until the estate agent goes back to his client to ensure that they are happy to allow the buyer to view at that budget.

What the buyer effectively is saying it that, even if they love the property, they cannot afford to pay over €500,000. The owners must then make a decision whether they can let the buyer view the property at that level. Either way, the buyer is gaining valuable market information that he would not have found on any property brochure.

Buyers may question why the seller would agree to this or allow it to happen. The most common reason seems to be because the estate agent's primary goal is to get buyers inside the property. If buyers do not view a property, there is no chance of them buying it (except in the case of foreign investors) so it is not in the estate agent's interest to keep the buyer out unless the property is genuinely outside of the stated budget. Going back to the previous analogy, the estate agent will never get to wear his negotiator's hat unless the buyers see him in his sales' hat!

The downside of this strategy is that it demands a lot of hard work, research and cold calling by buyers as it may take 35 "No's" before they get their first "Yes". The good news, however, is that they should be well rewarded for the effort they put in. Every minute spent doing their property market homework should yield thousands of euro in savings.

The principal notion of pre-negotiation is not simply to knock a few thousand euro off the asking price, but rather for the buyer to secure a lot more property for their budget. This is the best way to acquire *positive* equity in the property they buy, thus avoiding any risk of negative equity in the short and medium term.

Pre-negotiations – A Case Study

Maria, aged 38, was a cash buyer in the north Kildare area. She had separated from her partner in 2007 (no children) and they had sold their Dublin 7 home. After clearing the mortgage, each party received cash proceeds of €240,000. Maria also had savings of approximately €40,000 and was looking to purchase a home outright, that is, without any mortgage if possible. The difficulty with this search was that Maria was very flexible in terms of location. As a self-employed consultant with a client base in Dublin city centre and throughout Leinster, Maria's only criterion was access to the M50 and M7 motorways.

After agreeing to a cash budget of €250,000 for a completed or habitable two to three bedroom house, Maria, with assistance, then carried out a search of the north Kildare, west Dublin and west Wicklow areas. The number of potential properties was over 780. This list was narrowed down by ruling out the least preferred areas, property types and conditions having regard to the self-applied budget – that is, up to €400,000.

Having done this, Maria was still left with approximately 125 potentially suitable properties. This was too huge a volume to consider viewing all, so Maria started to work through the listings in groups of estate agents – that is, looking at all of the properties with one particular firm. She then made contact with each firm and discussed the selection of properties. Conversations with the estate agents provided enough information for Maria to rule out properties that were in need of a greater level of work than she was prepared to carry out, or those under offer or whose owners had already rejected offers of a certain value. By doing this, she whittled down the list of 125 properties to 10 to 15 that were priced to sell and whose owners were prepared to financially reward an early cash buyer. Most importantly, this ruled out properties not achievable within budget. Out of the remaining properties, Maria viewed approximately 10 and made an offer on two of the most suitable. As it happens, both offers were accepted and Maria elected to proceed with the purchase of a 1970s bungalow on a half-acre in north Kildare. The bungalow was in need of upgrading but was entirely habitable and Maria was in a position to purchase it outright for €230,000 (guide price was €299,000) and start the upgrading works herself.

If Maria had used conventional search methods – that is, no pre-negotiation – she might have had to view up to 780 properties to find this seller and this property.

KEY POINTS FROM CHAPTER 11

❖ The concept of property pre-negotiation was introduced by property buyers' brokers in an attempt to identify the quality properties and motivated sellers from the high volume of stock that existed in the Irish market.

❖ It involves negotiating the property within a certain price range *prior* to viewing it.

❖ This works as a strategy as the viewings are contingent on successful negotiation in advance.

❖ The notion behind pre-negotiating is to move away from questionable sales techniques, or 'tricks of the trade', employed by some estate agents. *Tricks are illusions; therefore any results will be illusions, that is, not real.* Buyers must demand real value and real service within the marketplace.

Chapter 12

STRATEGIC SELECTION

Assess the property on paper

It is far more effective for a buyer to focus their energy on researching a large selection of properties and then only viewing the best. This volume of research increases the buyer's knowledge of the market and their capability to assess value on a locally comparative basis. The more time spent investigating the offerings of the market leads to better, more informed decision-making by the buyer, whereas excessive viewings can cause property blindness. That is to say, buyers will become overwhelmed by the volume, under-whelmed by the sameness of the properties and ultimately frustrated by the entire house-hunting process. As that stage, they are much less likely to recognise a good deal or a quality property when they find it. When it comes to viewings, think of the words of Audrey Hepburn as Sabrina Fair when she declares, "More isn't always better, you know. Sometimes, it's just more".

As referred to throughout this handbook, buying property is a process and each step along the way must be considered a separate part of it, a mini-process of sorts. For this reason, buyers are advised to keep a list of all the properties they have noted, researched and pre-negotiated. This does not have to be anything too sophisticated – just scribbling in a notebook or on their computer will help buyers to document the search, list pros and cons for each property and jot down any points of note. Buyers should not be tempted to cheat by merely using an account on one property website to save properties as it will distort the findings.

This list should be an ongoing account of the properties and their features, both positive and negative. With this in place, buyers will be able to see at a glance what properties can be pre-negotiated within budget, and compare the features of each against the buyer's own search criteria.

The idea is to rate the properties in order of suitability so that only the very best value and most suitable homes are viewed. Using this technique will save buyers the time and stress associated with unsuccessful viewings. For example, if buyers know that they need a large garden space for the family dog, and this is a non-negotiable requirement, then they should not view a property that features a 'city space' or 'compact BBQ area', as these are euphemisms for 'this property has no garden'. The worst thing that can happen to the buyer in this instance is to fall in love with the property, the layout, its interior design and so on. The buyer will then agonise over the garden issue before sensibly realising that no border collie can sleep in a barbeque pit. Unfortunately, this property will now haunt the buyer for the remainder of the search, and every new property will be compared to it. This is a point of frustration for the buyer, not to mention for the estate agent. The moral of this story for buyers is not to view properties that feature known deal-breakers.

In the current market, the huge volume of properties available will make it more difficult for buyers to narrow down their selection, which is why the buyers' list will be instrumental. The most effective way for the buyer to put together this list is to define what they need and want to achieve from the property. For most buyers, these needs can be categorised as a *lifestyle* need or a *financial need*, as illustrated below.

Lifestyle Needs

Size

The size of the property sought or the space needed will depend upon the buyer's and/or family's requirements. This might be a minimum number of bedrooms or above average living space to accommodate a home office. Unlike location, this may be quite a flexible feature as often with houses there is room to extend. This will interest buyers whose budgets do not allow for the size property they need in certain areas. It is worth remembering that not all development requires planning. Buyers are advised to check out the Exempt Development guidelines to see whether extension work might be undertaken without the need for a formal application. Exempt Development applies to extensions of up to 40 square metres on the ground floor and 12 square metres at first floor level, subject to the height of the roof and distances from neighbouring properties.

Property Type
The buyer usually will have a clear idea of the type of property they require, that is, whether a house or an apartment. In terms of houses, the buyer most likely will have a preference for either a new, modern home or perhaps an older property with special features and character. As sometimes happens, the property can be in conflict with the other needs of buyers – for example, the location: a converted cottage will be difficult to find in the suburbs.

Location
This will be a point of focus for every buyer. Commuting distance to work and schools is a big concern, as is proximity to services and facilities such as public transport, shopping centres and restaurants. Many buyers prefer to settle within familiar areas or close to family. Buyers are advised to find out about any plans for new transport possibilities – for example, trains, buses, roads, etc. – with the local planning office.

Financial Needs
Budget
One of the principal financial needs of the buyer, when selecting or short-listing properties, is for that property to come within their budget. The pre-negotiation process, however, ensures buyers that

all properties on their list are within their price range. By using this technique, buyers are free to concentrate on prioritising other needs.

Value

There is a general fear of financial misjudgement among buyers in the current market. Securing value for money is an absolute financial need for buyers, and the best way to achieve this is to secure the property below market value. The obvious difficulty posed for buyers is how to accurately assess that value to ensure they do not pay more than the property is worth. There are several methods of valuing property in Ireland, which are discussed fully in Chapter 13.

Equity

Equity is another key concern for current buyers. In simple terms, equity is the difference between the value of the property and the value of the mortgage secured upon it. Negative equity is a very real problem in Ireland at the moment, with an estimated 300,000 to 350,000 properties affected. Prospective home-buyers need to be confident that they can avoid this in the short term by buying well and future-proofing their new homes against further price drops.

There are three ways to acquire equity in a home:

- The first and most desirable way to achieve equity is to acquire it at the time of purchase. This means buying a property that is well below market value so that equity exists on it as purchased. In a falling or stagnant market, buying property can be a gamble; however, by selecting areas that are up and coming, buyers can improve their chances of success. When it comes to identifying improving areas, new infrastructural developments or additional public transport routes are positive signs that an area is moving in the right direction. If in doubt,

buyers can check with the local council planning office to
see if there are any improvements to these areas planned.

- The second way is for equity to occur naturally over time
  as the mortgage decreases and the value of the home
  increases. This has been the route to positive equity for
  most existing home-owners in the past, but it is less likely
  to be the route for new home-buyers in 2012/2013.

- The third way for buyers to acquire equity in their home is
  to add value. This can be done at any stage of ownership.
  The most common ways to add value to any residential
  property are to extend into the attic or garage space, kit
  out a home office (highly desirable in the current market);
  invest time or money in garden landscaping; upgrade the
  kitchen or give the property an eco-friendly energy make-
  over (grants available).

Having regards to the needs outlined above, each individual buyer
will have different priorities and each factor will be of weighted
importance. In order to maximise the chances of success with
fewer viewings and less time-wasting, buyers are advised to
identify the best six to eight properties and arrange to view them
all on one day. The steps for successful viewings are laid out in
Chapter 14.

KEY POINTS FROM CHAPTER 12

- ❖ After compiling lists of properties from both on- and off-
  market sources, and successfully pre-negotiating them,
  the buyer will be left with a (much reduced) list of
  available properties within budget.

- ❖ Excessive viewings, particularly of the wrong property,
  can limit a buyer's ability to spot the right property when
  it comes. For that reason, the list must be whittled down

to the best six to eight properties for viewing based on the lifestyle and financial needs of the buyer.

❖ Lifestyle needs/wants:

o Size of property based on family, etc.

o Property type, house or apartment

o Location – proximity to work, schools, family, facilities.

❖ Financial needs/wants:

o Must be within budget (achieved in advance through pre-negotiation)

o Value – in an uncertain market, value cannot be assumed and buyers need to buy well in order to protect against future drops in the market

o Equity – that is, the balance in the property when the mortgage is deducted from the market value.

Chapter 13

METHODS OF VALUATION

What is it worth?

The dissolution of the 30th Dáil in January 2011 was heralded as a welcome political development for the nation, but it came at an additional cost to would-be home-buyers. Various crises and political turmoil, particularly since mid-2010, meant that the Minister for Justice & Law Reform was unable to introduce an amendment to the *Property Services Bill* to establish a National Property Price Register. This failure flies in the face of assurances given to lobbying bodies across all sectors of the property industry, and frustrates the already cautious market, arguably setting it back even further.

In an eleventh-hour attempt to stimulate the property market the stamp duty regime was reformed in the *Finance Bill 2011*, widening the net so that all buyers are now liable, but reducing the rates so that moving is no longer cost-prohibitive. While this is a positive development for those buyers trading up or with cash to invest, it could be argued that this reform might have been more effective as a stimulus initiative in 2012 or 2013, when confidence has increased to a point where cash buyers are willing to invest in the Irish property market. Stimulating the trading-up market should not have been a priority as this particular sector of the market was surviving; not booming, but certainly surviving. This premise is supported by Exchequer returns showing an increase in stamp duty of 38 per cent in 2010 over the previous year and a further increase of 45 per cent for 2011. Armed with this evidence (which is as close to market data as can accurately be obtained), the market would have been better served by creating the National Property Price Register as a priority and announcing a lead-in time for the stamp duty changes. This would have had a more pronounced effect on the market as it would have motivated any undecided, first-time buyers who were sitting on the fence, and it would have allowed their decision to be an informed one. It also would have made greater sense in terms of access to available credit and dealing with current stock levels around the country as first-time buyers are still the borrowers of choice. This class of buyer consumes the so-called 'starter home' of the past, thereby freeing up the next wave of buyers, those trading up, in time for 2012 or 2013 when stamp duty reform would have been most effective.

Instead, Ireland is left with a system of property valuation that is laughingly referred to as an 'art form rather than a science' by even the most experienced valuation professionals. This is simply not good enough for buyers. Uncertainty in the market is preying on the minds of would-be buyers, who are terrified of the financial risk. In particular, they fear paying more than the property is worth and finding themselves in negative equity. To return to the market, buyers must feel a real sense of confidence in the value to be achieved, and while this is best done by providing reliable market data, there are some methods that buyers can apply when assessing value in the absence of a National Property Price Register.

There are several acceptable methods of valuation of residential property in Ireland, though none are infallible. The valuation methodology tends to change depending on whether it is being applied to building, buying or selling a property for personal use or as an investment. Confusion arises when different methods of valuation result in very different values being placed on the property. The most applicable valuations for residential buyers are the *comparative*, *repayment* and *investment* methods. The cost methods, or *base value* of a property, will be applied to the cost of building the property. The *residual value* calculation is popularly applied by developers when acquiring sites to develop.

Comparative Valuation Method

The comparative method is exactly how it sounds: using the past sales price of a similar property to value another. Worryingly, this is the method that most influences values in Ireland, despite the lack of accurate sales price data in the country. The valuer looks at available data, typically sales by their own office, anecdotal industry discussion and reports from property sales websites. As a result, the so-called value is distorted by the levels of sales within a particular estate agency office, the efforts of sales personnel within the office and the sometimes aspirational and sometimes strategic asking prices of competing firms. Professionals regularly refer to this as 'open market value'; however, for this to be a genuine, reliable indicator, it must be based on actual *achieved* property prices, and in Ireland there is only a snapshot of this through public auctions and the mortgage data trends. Obviously, this does not tell a buyer much about one particular road or street over another, and it fails to take into consideration off-market cash purchases at all.

Sample Property

Take as an example a two bedroom house in Dublin 1, which is derelict and in a poor state of repair. Situated in an area experiencing an intensive level of regeneration, there are many newly-built, commercial buildings in the immediate area. Neighbouring properties sold in the boom years and are now part commercial/part residential with roof terraces. Located on a narrow street, there is no parking in the immediate vicinity. There is a newly built, multi-storey car park just opposite.

The guide price is €170,000, but pre-negotiation assures the well-researched buyer that the property can be secured for approximately €130,000 to €140,000. The level of discount is based on the seller's need to sell and the property being unsuitable for financing through a mortgage unless the buyer has cash reserves of at least €60,000 to carry out necessary repairs.

If the property was upgraded and subsequently let to tenants, a monthly rent of €1,300 would be expected in the current market.

Buyers trying to assess the value of the above property using the comparative valuation method would have to investigate competing properties on the open market, and then speak to other local estate agents or buyers' brokers to find out what level of sales has been achieved in the recent past. Due regard also will need to be made to the difficulty in raising finance on this property and the status of the area – that is, that it *is experiencing*, not that it *has experienced,* intensive regeneration. In the current cycle, the property market has been in a prolonged downward trajectory and is now only reaching stabilisation in highly desirable areas; stabilisation in areas of higher risk may take much longer to see. A buyer must realise that that area is unlikely to improve over the course of the next cycle (typically seven to 10 years) due to expected low levels of development and further regeneration. Therefore, investing in up and coming areas requires a long-term view – does this suit the buyer at this time? Positives to consider are the city centre location, commercial activity in the area and the potential to develop the house into a stylish, modern and ultimately valuable home.

Repayment Valuation Method

Another method of valuation is the repayment option, which aims to repay or recoup the price of a property within a defined period, usually 15 years. The 15-year timeframe is based on a commercial mortgage rather than a residential mortgage – that is, it is based upon the likely income that could be derived from the property if for whatever reason the buyer could not remain there and had to rent to tenants. This method of valuation is more effective for commercial property as it does not take into consideration the desirability of the area and other priorities for homeowners. Fastidious buyers of late have been applying this method of valuation to potential homes and finding a huge gap between the calculated repayment value and the estate agents' guide price. This may be due, in part, to the property being over-valued, but it is also caused by applying an unsuitable method of valuation.

Using the sample property in the example above, the repayment valuation would be applied as follows:

€1,300 (monthly rent) x 12 (months) x 20 years (term of residential mortgage) = Valuation of €312,000[1]

Investment Valuation

An investment valuation is calculated using the likely yield from the property. The standard test has always been to aim for a percentage yield of no less than the cost of borrowing. In the past that figure was upwards of 3 per cent, but in the current market 5 per cent is the minimum expected. The likely annual rents achievable are expressed as a percentage of the asking price. A higher yield means a greater level of return. For homebuyers, covering the cost of borrowings is a solid test, particularly in an uncertain market where the future is less than secure. Investors would be looking for an element of profit over and above the cost of borrowings.

Once again, using the sample property, the investment valuation would be applied as follows:

€1,300 (monthly rent) x 12 (months) – Yield calculation of 8% = €195,000 (price and works)

---

[1]   Buyers should note that these valuations are for demonstrative purposes only. In a detailed analysis, buyers also would consider the cost of borrowings, purchasing expenses, tax liabilities, on-going maintenance and repair costs of the property.

Even using a relatively high yield of 8 per cent (anything above 6 per cent in the current market makes investing worthwhile), the valuation of the property when completed is calculated at €195,000.

Base Valuation

The base valuation of a property is reached by calculating the costs of the site together with the cost of building. This is most typically used by those buyers considering self-building their home. The base value is usually compared with likely market value upon completion to decide whether the project makes sense financially. The base value also is used, in part, to assess the reinstatement value for the purposes of insuring the property.

Residual Valuation

The residual method of valuing property is rarely used, or encouraged for use, by home-buyers. It is most commonly used by developers to assess the likely profits from property, usually development land. It is calculated by taking the estimated value of the proposed development when completed, and deducting the cost of developing, including profits. The residual sum is taken to be the current, real value.

In general, residential property in Ireland is not subjected to any scientific formulae based on any single methodology but rather the valuer's professional opinion of what price is likely to be achieved on the open market within a reasonable period of time, in reasonable market conditions. The most effective method of valuation will differ depending upon the property type; however, for most buyers, a multi-faceted approach to valuation will provide the best results.

Factors to be considered when assessing the likely value of a new home are:

1. The percentage fall in prices from the peak. Remember that 50 per cent is a national average, but drops range from 30 per cent

to 75 and even 80 per cent depending upon the area. Buyers must do their research.

2. The total *relevant* stock sitting on the immediate/local market. If an apartment is not desirable, it ought not to be included in the calculations.

3. The likely yield on property, as calculated above. Circumstances may change over the short term, particularly in the current market, and buyers must be able to manage the mortgage shortfall. Other factors affect value – for example, the status and desirability of the area. Are there any plans to attract investment? Are works underway to extend existing public transport links? Buyers can speak to the local council to find out about plans.

KEY POINTS FROM CHAPTER 13

❖ The current government failed to introduce the long-promised amendment to the *Property Services Bill*, which was needed to establish a National House Price Register. As a result, the Irish market still does not have access to comprehensive, accurate data upon which to base valuations. However, this register is expected by mid-2012.

❖ In the absence of this, acceptable methods are as follows:
  o Comparative valuation method
  o Repayment valuation method
  o Investment valuation method
  o Base valuation
  o Residual valuation.

❖ In the current uncertain market, buyers are advised to take a multi-faceted approach to valuing property based on the following:
  o Percentage price drop

- o Likely yield achievable
- o Current relevant stock levels locally
- o Other factors of desirability – for example, status and desirability of the area.

Chapter 14

SUCCESSFUL VIEWING

Know the right questions to ask

Too many buyers, using traditional but flawed thinking, look upon viewing property as part of the negotiation process, which it is not. It is research. They do not need to negotiate on the day of the viewing because, if they followed the strategy in Chapter 11, they already will have pre-negotiated the price within a certain range, and by doing so they already know that the property can be secured within budget. Viewings are not about playing games; they are about finding out whether a particular property is the right one for the buyer.

Once the buyer has made an appointment to view the property, it is strongly recommended that he conducts a drive-by the night before. Not only will the buyer get a better sense of the neighbourhood after dark, but it will tell him a lot about the habits of the neighbours. In particular, he will see how cooperative the parking situation is when everyone is home from work and maybe receiving visitors. Also, he will see whether there are any youths hanging around the green areas. In fact, this is the type of social issue that can actually be pinpointed in advance, particularly in newer developments. It can be said, albeit flippantly, that children devalue a neighbourhood, though of course what is referred to here is the early detection of likely future social problems. In a new estate, most occupiers are young families so the buyer is unlikely to find teenagers hanging around; however, if he sees children's toys left to rust or rot in the green area and unaccompanied toddlers in his path as he reverses his car, this could be highly

Camera.

indicative of future anti-social issues as those toddlers grow. This is not being elitist or putting forth negative stereotypes, it is reality. A buyer is committing himself financially to this area so he must make a conscious, well-informed decision.

As at every stage of the buying process, preparation is essential. It is a myth that the more often a person views a house, the more likely they are to spot potential problems before they move in. That is absolute nonsense. The buyer should certainly be able to carry out a full assessment of the property, its benefits and its potential pitfalls on the first viewing if they pay attention and focus on the task in hand. It is much easier to do this with a prepared mind so buyers are advised to have a printed checklist of things to watch out for and questions that they need to ask the owner or estate agent.

When buyers arrive for a viewing, they should try to arrive a few minutes early so that they can check out the area in the daytime; most people are surprised at the difference a few hours can make. Last night's parking chaos might now give way to the look of a ghost estate, particularly in areas where young working couples reside.

Arriving early also helps the buyer to check out the exterior of the property. The buyer should not panic – he does not need to be a structural engineer for this. If the viewing is successful, buyers are strongly recommended to engage the services of a registered structural surveyor (covered in Chapter 17) to report on the property before they buy it; however, there are other defects that they should be watching out for themselves. There is little point in wasting money on a survey if the buyer already can see that the property is in poor condition and they do not have a budget for renovation.

A UK study carried out in 2009 revealed that up to 25 per cent of homeowners found a problem with their new home after they had moved in. Latent issues included, but were not limited to, poor heating, damp, badly-fitted windows/doors, lack of insulation and environmental issues like noise. Some of the affected homeowners felt that the problems had been deliberately hidden from them, but most admitted that it had not even occurred to them to look! It is reasonable to expect that Irish purchasers have experienced similar levels of post-purchase trouble.

Buyers are advised first to evaluate the exterior of the property – just cross to the opposite side of the road so that they can get a good overview of the house in relation to neighbouring units.

Buyers then are advised to check for evidence of the following:

1. Does the property need repainting?
2. Is there worn or cracked brickwork?
3. Is the roofline sagging?
4. Are there any roof tiles missing?
5. Are the chimneys shared, as in the case of some terraced properties?
6. Are the chimneys straight?
7. Is the lead flashing intact and secure?
8. Do the drains and guttering look old, damaged or blocked?
9. Are the fascias in good condition?
10. Are the windows double-glazed?
11. Does there appear to be a working alarm system?
12. Are there any apparent security risks?

Once again, buyers should pay attention to the details inside the property. Some things to watch out for are listed below, and anything serious should be inspected by the surveyor if the buyer decides to make an offer:

1. Is the level of redecoration required acceptable?
2. Is the property excessively warm or cold as they enter?
3. Is there any condensation or signs of damp? Check for fresh paint.
4. Are there cracks in the walls? Check for signs of cover-up.

5. Do all windows and doors open and close without pressure?

6. Any evidence of leaks, damp patches on the ceilings?

7. What is the condition of the flooring, particularly beneath first-floor carpeting?

8. Do all lights work?

9. Do the electrics have modern fittings?

10. Will it be necessary to add or move power, phone or TV points?

11. Is there a working electric shower?

12. Do all toilets flush and do hot and cold taps all work?

13. Is there access to the attic? This is essential for the surveyor.

Buyers who spot a problem with anything listed above should not be put off. The best course of action is to ask the estate agent about it. Buyers should be careful not to make assumptions about the owner or estate agent – they are neither your friend nor your enemy, but simply doing their job. If the estate agent is aware of any defects to the property, he is not obliged to disclose them; however, he is obliged to answer any questions put to him in as open and honest a way as possible. More importantly, buyers need to really listen to the answers; it is simple but powerfully effective.

Below is a sample of some suggested questions to ask the estate agent during the viewing:

1. What work did the current owners undertake, and when?

2. What age is the boiler and is there a full service history?

3. Are the chimneys in working order?

4. What is the approximate age of the electrics?

5. What are the local refuse arrangements and fees?

6. Who uses the side/rear access lane?

Depending upon the responses the buyer get to any of the issues that arise, they should either treat the issue as a deal-breaker (only if it genuinely is), or note it for the surveyor to pay particular attention to and/or use it as an additional negotiating tool if they proceed with the purchase. Do not be tempted to try to 'value' it in terms of discount on the day. It will not be effective as a strategy and worse, it will antagonise the owner or estate agent at a time when the buyer might need their goodwill.

Following on from this point, if the property has benefits, the buyer should appreciate them. That sentence goes against the grain for many buyers, but again, it must be pointed out that the day of viewing is not the time for the buyer to pick an argument with the owner or agent over relatively minor defects in the hope that it will increase their negotiating power. In fact, to do so while standing in the property merely strengthens the estate agent's hand considerably.

Talking about goodwill in this context might seem unusual, but there is an element in the Irish psyche that inclines people to do business with *people* – that is, individuals. The same is true for sellers. They like to know who will be buying their property. As it is human nature, they will be more inclined to work with buyers they like, respect or can relate to, and the converse is also true. There are many instances of buyers who were successful in securing their new property because the seller connected with them and their particular situation. This is covered in greater detail in Chapter 15, where it becomes relevant during the offer process.

Below are some additional considerations for buyers when viewing apartments.

Features

- Privacy – this applies to both the apartment and within the development. Buyers should check for other apartments facing the main windows, obstructing any views or inhibiting privacy.
- Parking – anything less than two spaces probably will be unworkable. Buyers should clarify the position regarding visiting cars and check what level of security is in place.

- **Immediate neighbours** – this is a difficult one to police in advance but do ask questions and draw assumptions from the surroundings.
- Ceiling heights – in apartments, these need to be more generous than in houses; a minimum of 10 feet is advised.

Location

- Buyers are best to avoid 24-hour supermarkets where possible due to constant noise. Proximity to restaurants might have consequences in terms of parking and possibly pest control.
- While living within an older neighbourhood of terraced houses might seem quaint, buyers here generally are subject to a lifetime of ongoing renovations and Sunday morning construction projects.
- Busy main thoroughfares are to be avoided as windows will have to be kept closed to protect the owner or occupants from noise, dust and fumes.
- Proximity to derelict sites or wasteland will present two problems. In the short term it may attract anti-social behaviour, and in the long term future development is likely and there are no guarantees as to the nature of that development.

Watch out for

- Damp patches or water marks that indicate leakages.
- Water pressure is important and many apartments on the highest floors will suffer from poor pressure levels unless they are fitted with a pressure pump.
- Waste disposal system and facilities.
- The number of elevators and stairs.

Management company issues

- Buyers must assess the performance of the management company to date, which can be done by looking through documents and accounts that accompany contracts for sale, but at the time of viewing the condition of the development will tell buyers a great deal.

- Ensure that there is a sinking fund[2] in place, find out how much is it worth currently and what works have been carried out to date or planned for the future.

- The annual management company fees need to be taken into consideration. More importantly, any prospective buyer must clarify what services or benefits the apartment owner and the development actually get for the fees paid.

KEY POINTS FROM CHAPTER 14

❖ Drive by the property in advance of the viewing, preferably at night, to get a true picture of the neighbourhood.

❖ Arrive early for the viewing to assess the exterior fully.

❖ Work off a checklist and make a note of any interesting features or comments that the estate agent might make.

❖ Know the right questions to ask an estate agent to ensure full disclosure.

❖ If the property has positive features, it is okay to appreciate them.

---

[2]   A provision for management company expenditure of a non-recurring nature.

Chapter 15

THE OFFER PROCESS

It is not all about the price

The offer process is one of the most daunting aspects of buying a property for many buyers; however, it does not need to be. In fact, the offer process, when managed correctly, actually can aid negotiations. The important point for buyers to remember is that price is just one factor that will be considered by the seller. It is usually the most important factor, but the overall proposal may not necessarily hinge on money once the buyer is within the right price range.

Buyers who followed the pre-negotiations strategy discussed in Chapter 11 will really feel the benefits here as they already will know about the sellers' circumstances and the likely price range that they are willing to accept. There are a few golden rules that may be applied by the buyer to ensure a successful outcome, however it should be noted that each transaction will vary so buyers should take a sensible approach to making an offer.

Best practice guidelines are as follows:

1. **Start low**. This will not surprise too many buyers! The advice to start low is not given because it is a good strategy, but because the seller and their estate agent expect it. In time, when the market evolves further, it should be possible for the buyer to offer the price that he feels the property is worth to him – until then a merry dance is required, though this can be minimised by a tight pre-negotiation. To be clear, starting low in this instance refers to the lowest price within the price range

– buyers will not do themselves any favours by viewing the house at a discounted, pre-negotiated price and then putting in an offer substantially below that. Not only will it be rejected, but the buyer may have alienated the seller to such a point that he would rather sell to anyone else even at a lower price.

2. **Always in writing.** This probably could have been the title of this handbook, and will certainly appear in most chapters. It is crucial for the buyer to put forward the offer to the seller or the estate agent in writing. This protects the buyer and eliminates any miscommunication. This is usually done by way of an email to the estate agent setting out the amount of the offer, together with the terms upon which the offer is made, for example, if it is time-restricted.

3. **Subject to structural survey.** It is always recommended that buyers engage the services of a qualified surveyor / building engineer to examine the property for any structural defects. Any offer should be made subject to a structural survey. This does not count as a conditional offer in the way that property chains or subject to finance is. Structural survey is covered in Chapter 17.

4. **Time limit.** A timed offer allows the buyer to take back control of the process from the seller. It also helps to focus the seller's mind on the offer – that is to say, the seller cannot wait for weeks and use the offer as leverage to pressure other buyers. The offer should be valid for a period of 48 to 72 hours, unless the sellers are outside of Ireland or the estate agent does not have easy access to them, in which case one week might be appropriate. An offer that is not accepted during that time frame is deemed to be rejected.

5. **Sell yourself.** As mentioned, the price is just one factor for sellers to consider; access to finance, quick decision-making and the buyer's ability to close the deal will all help the seller assess whether the offer is coming from a genuine buyer. These qualities of the buyer might compensate somewhat for a low

offer; for example, generally a seller who wants to sell quickly will accept a lower offer from a committed, ready buyer than from an investor who has offers on several properties at the same time.

6. **One at a time.** It is an acceptable practice to put an offer on more than one property at the same time, a tactic commonly used by investors. However, as a strategy, it is not very effective. The element of competition does not pressure the seller into accepting the offer; in fact, it may put the seller off as he will know that the buyer is not committed to securing this particular property. By only putting an offer on one property at a time, but applying a strict time limit, buyers let sellers know that if they accept then the deal will go through.

7. **Do not make threats.** Buyers are advised not to make threats unless they are willing to follow through. For example, the buyers should not refer to an offer as their *final* offer if it is not, as they will lose all credibility with the estate agent.

It is essential to get the written offer right first time. It is worthwhile for buyers to take their time in drafting this email or letter as mistakes may prove costly to rectify later. Below is a sample offer, which will need to be modified in accordance with the particular property and circumstances:

Subject to Contract/Contract Denied

Re: Address of the property

Dear Estate Agent,

Further to our recent viewings at the above property and to our subsequent telephone conversations, I would like to put forward an offer to purchase this property for €XXX,000. This offer is subject to a structural survey which will be arranged immediately upon your clients' acceptance of this offer.

---

good.

As a first-time buyer, I do not have flexibility on price but I can confirm that my mortgage is in place and I am willing to sign contracts and complete without delay, at your clients' convenience.

I can further confirm that I am not actively pursuing any other properties at this time. For that reason, I need to limit the time period that this offer can remain valid and I would be obliged to receive your clients' response to this offer no later than (date).

I look forward to hearing from you further.

Kind regards,

The Buyer

If the offer has been rejected by the estate agent, or if the estate agent has failed to respond within the prescribed timeframe, the offer is negated. While the seller or estate agent may come back after a few weeks, the buyer has no obligation to engage in further discussions. Of course, if the estate agent is coming back to say that the offer (that no longer applies) has been accepted, the buyer might want to consider putting in another offer but at a slightly discounted rate.

Another fear that buyers have is the threat of being 'gazumped'. Gazumping is when a seller consents to a sale at an agreed price and then tells the buyer before contracts are signed that somebody else has offered more money and that they are going to sell to that other person instead. While not illegal in Ireland, it is considered poor practice and somewhat underhanded. Fortunately, it has never been particularly common in Ireland, and is much less common in the current market. It is an absolute myth that estate agents encourage this practice to increase fees; in reality, the percentage the estate agent makes on the increased offer is less than the price of a meal! No estate agent is foolish enough to lose a potential buyer in this manner. In the current market, where estate agents have more properties than buyers, they will not set buyers up to compete for the same property. Even if the strategy is successful, there is just one sale. It is far more likely that the estate agent will show the two buyers two different properties, thereby doubling his chances of success. This might come as a revelation to sellers, but it is the current reality.

Dealing with Competing Bids and Suspected False Bids

False bidding is a practice that is still prevalent in the industry and buyers have a real fear of it. There are measures, however, that buyers can take to ensure that they are not bidding against themselves. For instance, when the buyer is advised that there is an offer in place, usually at the viewing stage, it is sensible for the buyer to ask the estate agent the following:

1. When was the purported offer made? If it was not made within the last two to three weeks, disregard it. The seller may or may not realise it, but the other bidder most likely has moved on to another property by now.

2. How much is the offer for? This is important, but the buyer should only be influenced by it if it can be verified.

3. Is the other offer unconditional? If the other offer is conditional upon any event – for example, sale of their existing home or obtaining finance – the buyer is advised to disregard it.

4. What is the status of the offer? If the offer was made, the owner's response will be very telling. If the offer was accepted, the estate agent should not be considering further bids at this time. If the offer was rejected, buyers should ask why. It might not necessarily have been due to the amount – perhaps the bidders could not complete in time, or they attached onerous terms and conditions that were unacceptable to the seller. If, on the other hand, the offer is under consideration, the buyer knows that the offer figure falls within the likely price range at which the owner is willing to sell.

5. As always, ask the estate agent to confirm all his responses to the above questions in writing.

If there is a genuine, unconditional offer, the estate agent should have no difficulty in confirming all of these facts in an email. If that email is not forthcoming for any reason, the buyer can simply commit all the information to an email and send it to the estate agent. The email should read:

> 'Dear agent, I understand from our recent conversation that XXX property is currently subject to an unconditional offer of €XXX,000. Kindly confirm same.'

Confirmation from the estate agent now requires a simple one word email: 'confirmed'. Once the buyer has this confirmation, they can take it that the other offer is genuinely as presented. Of course, if the buyer finds that they are dealing with a particularly obtuse agent who refuses to give confirmation of the facts above, they either can walk away from the property (and that estate agent) or disregard the competing bid and act as if there was no offer on the property, which is most likely the case.

What often happens next is a bit of blustering, maybe some backtracking, and an explanation from the estate agent that the other offer in fact was conditional upon that party selling their existing home in Tipperary, or securing finance, or some other obscure event in the future that may never happen. What this effectively means is that there was no valid offer in place (note that it may take a while to get to this point!).

The power of committing this type of information to paper (or electronic form) is quite real. Estate agents are licensed and, in most cases, (self-)regulated professionals. They are engaged by the seller and must represent the seller at all times. Their only duty towards the buyer is to act in an ethical manner and answer any questions truthfully, which makes it essential for buyers to know the right questions to ask. While getting truthful answers is difficult to be sure of if the communication is verbal, it is very straightforward when the communication is written. As a rule, no professional will compromise the truth in a written response.

If there is a valid or verifiable competing offer that is conditional, buyers can make a lower, unconditional bid for the property, but should still make it subject to a strict time limit. Where buyers are faced with an unconditional competing bid, they simply must decide whether the property is worth pursuing or competing for (post-offer negotiations are discussed in Chapter 16). If it is worth pursuing, buyers should determine the price level at which they are prepared to compete (a cut-off price); if not, the best advice is to walk away and look for another property. This is a buyer's market after all!

KEY POINTS FROM CHAPTER 15

- ❖ When it comes time to making an offer, it is not all about price. The buyer needs to sell themselves to the seller, to make the seller want to sell to them over other buyers.
- ❖ Essentials of the offer process:
  - o Start low, not because it works but because it is expected!
  - o Always communicate in writing
  - o Offer is subject to a structural survey
  - o There is a time limit
  - o Do not make threats.
- ❖ If buyers feel they are competing with false bids, take control of the process and request confirmation of any other offers in writing.

Chapter 16

OPENING NEGOTIATIONS

Avoid dated practices that no longer work

In the earlier chapter on pre-negotiations, buyers were shown how to whittle down a list of potential properties to just a handful of below market value (BMV) opportunities by shaking out the motivated sellers from the rest. It is a painstaking process by any standards, but one that yields outstanding results using only the honest and ethical tactics of research, effort and strategy.

The success of pre-negotiation is largely attributable to the buyer turning the traditional buyer/seller relationship on its head by negotiating *prior* to viewing, and making any subsequent viewing contingent on a discounted price; therefore, viewing will take place only if the pre-negotiation is successful. The buyer is thus in a position of advantage throughout every stage of the process. By adopting this method of selecting properties, the buyer has a very clear idea of what the seller is likely to accept (within a certain price range) at the time of viewing. Using that price range, an offer can be made. Only in exceptional circumstances will the offer be accepted by the seller straight away – even if it is actually *acceptable* to the seller, they are unlikely to accept it without trying to get more. This is all part of any commercial arrangement. There are two parties, a buyer and a seller. Each must look out for their own interests.

At the start of every negotiation, each party has an advantage. At this stage of the process, the buyer's advantage is that they are now negotiating within a specified price range – that is, the starting offer up to the pre-negotiation figure, give or take a little.

From this point on, the top of this price range will be considered the 'walk away' price and the buyer cannot exceed it. The seller's advantage is the certain knowledge that the buyer wants to acquire this property. Even though the seller knows the pre-negotiated price, they may not believe it to be the 'walk away price' that will push the buyer away; this is a risk for the seller but it is one that most will take to achieve a higher price. This is where the traditional negotiation takes place and, therefore, where traditional mistakes get made by the buyer. But this does not have to be the case. The research has been done, the offer is in place and, with some sensible behaviour by both parties, a mutually acceptable deal can be struck. But first, it is back to basics: Negotiations 101.

There are different styles and classes of negotiations in property as in life. For success, it is crucial to use the right class of negotiation and the buyer must adapt their style to suit the circumstances of the seller and/or the estate agent.

Despite popular misconceptions, in property negotiations a 'plunder' approach is not likely to be successful (unless the seller is extremely distressed, and even then, there are more effective ways to negotiate with a strong hand). The strongest negotiation tactic is to 'read' people and situations, which comes from real-life interactions rather than theory so each encounter will enhance the buyer's skills. While a professional negotiator may have an advantage in terms of experience and skill, the buyers bring with them the simple but powerful advantage of a potential sale for the estate agent. However, any advantage will be eliminated by lack of preparation, which is the cornerstone of all effective negotiation and should never be underestimated. So when dealing with an experienced estate agent, research can give buyers the necessary edge. In preparation, speak to as many people as possible, for example, competing estate agents, neighbouring home-owners or tenants, local shop owners or businesses in the area. Information is there to be had – the key for buyers is to ask the right questions.

Buyers are advised to keep the lines of communication open with the estate agent, while remembering that the agent works on behalf of the seller only. Buyers should never forget this. At every step of the negotiations, which could take minutes, hours, days or weeks (anything longer than that, buyers should probably walk away as the seller is obviously not motivated to sell), all conversations should be agreed and referred to in writing. Similar to the guidelines for making an offer discussed in the previous chapter, this is done very simply by emailing the estate agent and referring to the main points of the conversation. This ensures absolute clarity and highlights potential issues or misunderstandings before they turn into problems. The golden rule is that there are three sides to every story: the buyer's, the seller's and the truth or reality which usually lies somewhere between the two. Usually neither has set out deliberately to deceive, they are simply mis-communicating – failing to understand each other and failing to make themselves understood. This is avoided by a brief follow-up email, which should be done as a matter of course with every new offer and the response to it.

As noted earlier when making an offer, with negotiation the buyer must start low – not because it is a smart tactic, but because the estate agent expects it. The pre-negotiation technique trumps this for purchase price, but for any extras and favourable contract terms it is worth remembering that a person will never get more than they asked for in a negotiation!

As a general rule, the buyer should be willing to listen to the estate agent, even if the price is not where it needs to be. The seller already has made a concession by agreeing to a discount in advance. The buyer needs to show that they are ready, willing and able to make the deal work. When negotiating the price range, never split the difference, as is generally suggested by one party when facing the wall. A better alternative is the well-established 'nickel and dime' approach. This is where the strong party concedes a smaller amount (the nickel, in this case) for every larger concession (the dime) that their counterpart offers. In practice, this would be where a buyer offers €450,000. The seller has agreed to a pre-negotiated figure of €500,000 so a counter-offer of €475,000 is put forward by the seller as a fair compromise. The buyer, who is in a position of strength (at the moment, this will not always be the case), does not accept this and agrees to €455,000 only. After much wrangling, the figure would most likely settle somewhere in the region of €460,000 to €465,000. By adopting the nickel and dime approach, the buyer has conceded €10,000 to €15,000, as opposed to the seller who has conceded €35,000 to €40,000.

In order for this to be successful, the buyer must give the seller something they want in exchange. For example, the seller might accept the sum of €460,000 on the condition that they can use the garden shed as storage for a period of six months and that the sale closes within a strict period of four weeks. Neither of these concessions is likely to bother the purchaser, who has just saved tens of thousands, and the seller can now commit to that around-the-world trip to kickstart their retirement in the certainty that the house is sold and their contents safely stored until they return. The result is a deal that did not focus solely on money but on other factors that were important to the seller. To see a deal brokered that satisfies both parties in unexpected ways reaffirms the old adage that bargaining is indeed more of an art than a science.

Negotiation Styles

To help inexperienced buyers through the ordeal of negotiations, it is useful to identify the styles of negotiators they are likely to encounter. This will also help buyers to recognise their own tendencies when negotiating.

The most common styles are:

- **Submissive**. A submissive negotiator is timid and more inclined to compromise or give large concessions. Unfortunately, inexperienced buyers fall into this category far more than estate agents do. They tend to be pleasant and forthcoming, but can be naïve about manipulative ploys.

- **Aggressive**. An aggressive negotiator is domineering and less inclined to give any concessions. This type of negotiator is unlikely to compromise, which damages a relationship. Negotiation is viewed as a win/lose process by this type. Trading on intimidation, aggressive negotiators know and use 'every trick in the book'.

- **A combination of the two**. This type of property negotiator is the one buyers will most likely come across. They are assertive and skilled at reading situations and people, but they are strong, tactical negotiators who never concede unless it is part of an overall strategy.

Difficult property negotiators are often overly aggressive in style, possibly ill-tempered and even ill-mannered in their dealings. Buyers will come across them so it is important that they can recognise and deal with this type successfully. They are often estate agents who are out of touch with the current market, have not come to terms with the changed trading environment and possibly feel quite threatened by this so-called buyers' market. In the past, their aggressive style may have intimidated buyers into accepting poor deals, which reinforces their belief that aggression makes them good negotiators. It is crucial, very early in the process, that buyers break this cycle by not giving in, but also by not engaging in combative responses themselves. Pre-negotiation is a great way to manage and lessen this type of behaviour by the estate agent. Buyers should just keep focused on the goals of the negotiation: to secure the ideal property and value-added extras at the best possible price. Be resolute in pursuing those goals.

The typical response by some sellers/estate agents to tough negotiations is to create competition for the buyer – sometimes this is real, but mostly it is not. This is unethical but, unfortunately, it does happen, although not as often as buyers fear. Knowledge is the most effective tool to counteract any undesirable tactics in the property market. Buyers who do their research and carry out extensive due diligence at preliminary stages should be able to skilfully out-manoeuvre this behaviour.

Bluffing is a skill, but one that can be learned. It can be dangerous and downright counter-productive, however, if used unwisely and without basis. A successful bluff is one based upon a factual position. A bluff is not to be mistaken for a threat, however. Buyers should not threaten to walk away if it is not their intention to do so as it makes further negotiations untenable.

In property negotiations, deadlines are crucial and should not be deferred without good reason. They force the seller to make decisions and keep the process within the control of the buyer to a certain extent. Time is a genuine pressure tool, but should not be over-used or used as a bluff. If time is used against the buyer, it is important to respond with two time plans: a long-term one and a short-term (conditional) one. Keep in close communication with the other party during the timed period.

Tactics aside, there are a few basic rules that buyers need to observe. For example:

- Demeanour in negotiations should be respectful towards the seller/estate agent at all times. This can be done while still maintaining strength.

- Emotion rarely should enter the negotiation process unless as part of some strategy, and even then one needs to be very careful.

- Indeed, lack of emotion is a great part of the skill that a professional negotiator brings to the table, and is one reason why sellers engage them on their behalf.

- Be selective in the use of negotiating language; for instance, 'we require', 'we need', 'we must have', 'we insist upon' are far more powerful than 'we would like', 'we wish', 'we hope for', or 'we request'.

- In the event that buyers find themselves dealing with an emotional seller, they should remain calm and focus on keeping control of the process. Buyers will have the upper hand in this case, so rather than exploit the weakness shown (which can be risky due to their unpredictable and volatile nature, and could result in the buyer losing the property), they should instead build on their own strengthened position.

- Buyers should avoid deliberately antagonising the seller or estate agent – even if it means occasionally biting their tongue!
- Buyers do not need to express their opinions on décor or furnishings; taste is subjective.

The most basic mistake that buyers make in the course of property negotiations is to question the estate agent's integrity without due cause. Unless they have given some reason to doubt them, this is disrespectful and antagonistic and will break down the very relationship that is needed to secure the property. The buyer needs the seller to agree to their offer, and the estate agent is the conduit for the seller. In this advanced stage of negotiations, no news is generally bad news for buyers, so regular communication between the buyer and seller can help keep the deal alive.

Finally, many negotiating experts talk about the 'golden bridge', which is basically a face-saving tactic (but an extremely important one as it may be the difference between closing a deal or not). In the context of a property negotiation, this involves giving the seller and/or his agent a way to professionally backtrack, concede and agree to an offer they had previously rejected. This can be done by introducing new terms, or highlighting previous ones (not financial) that are in favour of the seller. This is not derogatory or manipulative; it merely allows the seller to come back from their refusal without damaging the process. By allowing them to do this, the buyer makes it easier for the seller to concede.

Phase two negotiations effectively are completed when the seller accepts the offer put forward by the buyer. Again, this needs to be communicated in writing to ensure clarity on price, terms and conditions. As the offer (per Chapter 15) most likely was made subject to a structural survey, and this offer has now been accepted, the buyers should contact a qualified building surveyor or engineer to carry out this as soon as possible.

KEY POINTS FROM CHAPTER 16

- ❖ At the start of a negotiation, each party has an advantage. The buyer's advantage is that they are negotiating within a specified price range due to pre-negotiation; the seller's advantage is the knowledge that the buyer wants to acquire the property.

- ❖ Price negotiations are usually covered at the pre-negotiation stage so during closing buyers should push for added value extras.

- ❖ Never make an empty threat – if it is said, it should be meant. The buyer should ensure always that they are ready to walk away after that point.

- ❖ Be selective in the use of negotiating language and use forceful words rather than submissive ones.

- ❖ The 'golden bridge' is a face-saving tactic that allows the seller or their agent to backtrack in order to accept an offer that had previously been rejected.

Chapter 17

THE STRUCTURAL SURVEY

Why it is important and what to expect

The structural survey is a comprehensive inspection of the property in question, carried out by a qualified surveyor or engineer at the request of the potential home-buyer. It should not be confused with the lender's survey, which in reality is merely an independent valuation report. The purpose of the structural survey is to give the purchaser an unbiased evaluation of the overall condition of a property, and to highlight any aspects that may need repair, replacement or ongoing maintenance. Crucially, the report arising from the structural survey will provide the buyer with the information needed to make an informed decision on whether to go ahead with purchasing the property.

Unlike the bank survey, which is mandatory, a structural survey is optional, although any property professional would advise that the buyer undertake one before making the single, biggest investment of their life. Knowledge of defects or issues needing attention may discourage buyers from proceeding with the purchase outright, or may help to plan for work that is likely to be necessary in the short and medium term. Armed with this survey, the buyer should save a significant sum of money on defects that the seller may now have to correct before the sale is agreed. Knowing the cost of even small repairs, which can run to thousands of euro, can be a great negotiating tool.

Aspects of the property that are routinely checked in the course of structural survey are as follows:

External Areas	Internal Areas	Other
• Roof and chimneys • Guttering and flashing • Settlement cracks • Movement in foundations • Windows and doors • Drainage • Boundaries • Path and driveway.	• Interior attic space • Ceilings and floors • Interior walls • Windows and doors • Heating system • Plumbing and electrics • Working fireplaces • Ventilation and damp • Insulation.	• Compliance with Building Regulations.

There are some limitations to the survey, which may vary from one survey to another. Buyers will be made aware of these limitations by the surveyor, either in advance of the survey or within the report document. If there is any ambiguity, buyers are advised to seek clarification and not to assume anything.

The most notable limitations tend to be as follows:

- Roofs and chimneys in excess of three metres generally will be examined from ground level.
- The building fabric will not be breached in the course of the inspection. The survey is strictly on the basis of what is visible or accessible.
- Plumbing and heating systems will be activated where connection permits, but will not generally be tested unless there is reason to suspect a problem.
- Sewers are inspected to the extent of lifting covers on manholes. Once again, testing will only be recommended where there is some reason to suspect something.

The age of the building to be surveyed is a very important consideration. Buyers should not be fooled by a modern, well-finished home. The age is no guarantee of a sound structure. In fact, many experts maintain that the overall quality of new home construction over the past decade has deteriorated somewhat. Older houses have their own particular issues to contend with – for example, non-regulation windows or access – but they are generally well-constructed. When looking at the structural condition of the property, the engineer will pay particular attention to defects that are inconsistent with the age of the property. The engineer will issue a full report to the buyer, which will set out areas of the property needing attention and make recommendations.

Defects or areas needing attention may cause a re-negotiation of the purchase price. In addition, defects that are inconsistent with the age of the house should flag concern. For example, if the engineer finds a hole in the roof of a modern, three bedroom semi-detached house, a question mark may arise over the quality of the property. On that point, some buyers in the past have chosen not to request a structural survey where the house in question is less than 10 years old and covered under the original structural defect insurance scheme, usually Homebond. This is nonsense. Protection against defects for 10 years is of little benefit if the buyer cannot identify those defects.

It should be noted, however, that very few buildings are without any defects. The surveyor will furnish a lengthy report, many pages long, that will list observations, opinions and recommendations on issues that would not necessarily be classed as defects, so buyers should be prepared for this and not panic. When issues or possibly defects are identified, it does not necessarily mean that it is not a quality property. The buyer must work through the surveyor's report and determine which issues are consistent and to be expected, which issues are easily remedied and which issues are essentially deal-breakers. Whatever the outcome, knowing in advance is essential – forewarned is always forearmed.

Engineers' fees may vary, depending on the age and extent of the property, together with the location, or specifically, the time and travel involved. A survey generally will take between one to two hours. Buyers should expect to pay somewhere in the region of €350 to €450 plus VAT. If the buyer is waiting to sign contracts of sale, the engineer usually will give a verbal assessment of the property on the day of the survey – the equivalent to a thumbs up or thumbs down. The written report generally will issue within a period of five days.

By engaging a suitably qualified surveyor with professional indemnity insurance, buyers are assured that they are covered in the event that they suffer financial loss as a result of neglect, error or omission in the course of producing the structural survey.

Snag List

A snag list will be necessary for buyers purchasing a newly-built home. It is not a structural survey, as discussed above, but rather a checklist of minor defects that the builder or developer must complete prior to the sale closing. The vast majority of newly-built properties are covered by a building guarantee or under a structural guarantee scheme, such as Homebond or Premier, which protects the occupant of the home against specific significant defects for a period of 10 years. This protection applies to the property, not the owner; therefore, subsequent buyers will enjoy this protection for 10 years after the completion of the building.

The snag list consists of all the items that must be finished or fixed by the builder or developer before the sale is finalised. Builders have a poor reputation for after-sales service, so it is crucial that all outstanding items are dealt with before final monies are paid over. In certain circumstances, the sale might be allowed to proceed on the stated agreement of works to be carried out, but this leaves the buyer in a vulnerable position and is therefore not recommended. An exception to this might be the Irish weather causing huge delays in finishing the garden to specification. In this instance, the purchase might go ahead and close contracts subject to a small portion of the funds being withheld from the builder until such time as the garden works are completed.

As with the structural survey, a snag list is not mandatory, although it should definitely be regarded as essential by the new home-owners. Snag lists do not need to be carried out by a professional in order to be effective. In fact, some of the most comprehensive lists are carried out by the buyers, although engaging a professional engineer or surveyor has a number of benefits. Chiefly, their training and expertise suggests that they will uncover minor faults or needed finishing touches that the buyer might never have noticed. Secondly, they are likely to demand a higher quality finish than buyers might know to demand. Thirdly, buyers receive the benefit of professional indemnity insurance, as already discussed above. If any issue or defect is overlooked at the snagging stage, it may cost money to remedy it. By hiring a professional, that person is answerable to the buyer for any work carried out.

Buyers who have some experience in construction or who have purchased property previously might feel confident about compiling a thorough snag list themselves. If so, there is now a wealth of information available through Irish and UK websites, where buyers can read tips, learn from other buyers and download comprehensive DIY snagging checklists. One good resource is **www.snagging.org**. If there is reason for concern, however, buyers should speak to a qualified engineer.

KEY POINTS FROM CHAPTER 17

❖ The structural survey is an inspection of the property in question, carried out by a qualified surveyor for the potential home-buyer.

❖ It is not to be confused with the lender's survey, which is merely an independent valuation report.

- ❖ The purpose of the structural survey is to determine the condition of the property and to highlight any aspects that may need repair, replacement or ongoing maintenance.

- ❖ The structural survey will provide the buyer with the information needed to make an informed decision on whether to go ahead with purchasing the property.

- ❖ The buyer should be aware that older properties have inherent structural issues and these rarely will be considered deal-breakers. Buyers should be concerned about issues that are inconsistent with the age of the property.

- ❖ Further negotiations may take place to deal with issues arising from the report.

- ❖ A snag list consisting of all the items that must be finished or fixed by the builder or developer will be necessary for buyers purchasing a newly-built home.

Chapter 18

CLOSING NEGOTIATIONS

Your final chance to improve the deal

Upon receipt of the structural survey or report from the surveyor or engineer, many buyers panic. In fact, after reading many damning surveys, it is a constant surprise that the properties are still standing at all, such is the terror induced by the 16 to 20 page document. Many sales fall through as a result of inexperienced buyers failing to interpret the survey correctly and failing to understand the nature of the issues contained within. By taking the time to understand the report, buyers will see that the surveyor is comparing the property in question to the ideal standard. The surveyor's report generally will:

- Highlight existing issues or instances of non-compliance with building regulations
- Pinpoint areas that might be of concern in the future
- Make observations, and
- Make recommendations.

The purpose of the report is to let buyers know as much as possible about the structure today, while identifying likely future

prove necessary in the future. In many cases, this

aintenance of the building.

when faced with the structural survey, buyers will

ptions:

rom the purchase. Buyers should only

the purchase where there is a major structural

issue arising in the survey. Of particular note are issues inconsistent with the age of the building.

2. **Accept the contents of the report and proceed at the agreed price**. The reasonable position is that the offer to purchase was made subject to a *structural* survey and buyers should only re-negotiate the price if there is some structural issue that was hidden or not visible – for example, wood worm or dry rot. Some defects are inherent in older properties, like damp, ventilation or insulation issues. Buyers should discuss the report fully with their surveyor and seek clarification on areas of concern before making any decisions.

3. **Re-negotiate the agreed purchase price**. If there is a structural issue of genuine concern, then certainly the problem needs to be dealt with or the agreed price needs to be re-negotiated to reflect this issue.

This is phase three of negotiations, but in reality it is about problem-solving and it is likely the buyer and seller will be able to work together for mutual benefit. When it comes time to communicate the issues arising from the survey, the buyer may contact the estate agent directly or have his solicitor deal with the seller's solicitor. Experience suggests that a commission-hungry estate agent invariably will be more efficient at moving these matters on and finding resolution for the situation than a solicitor. Sellers generally will not approach this type of late negotiation with any level of goodwill if they feel that they have already been knocked down on price, so this is, perhaps, the most difficult phase for buyers to achieve savings. The buyer must put together a comprehensive list of the necessary work required, together with projected costs, and present this to the seller. As these quotes/estimates need to be sourced from different professionals, this may take a number of days or even weeks. In a more buoyant market, the seller would merely re-advertise the property and attract new buyers. In the current market, buyers will be in a stronger position, but should not abuse this position by delaying the process. When the final costs are collated, the buyer will be ready to put in an unconditional offer, reduced by the cost of the required work.

The negotiations here are more complex as both parties have invested time, energy and money in each other by this point in the process. As mentioned, problem-solving here is the focus rather than re-negotiation. The basic propositions remain the same: the purchaser wants to buy and is prepared to buy; the vendor wants to sell and is prepared to sell. Unfortunately for both parties, the survey has introduced a problem.

Positions

Buyer: The buyer has secured a great deal and wants to complete.
Seller: The seller too wants to complete but the structural issues are his problem to deal with.

Reality

Buyer: The price has effectively increased for the buyer who was financing the purchase up to his maximum budget. He simply cannot afford to complete as there are no further funds to carry out the work needed.
Seller: The seller is in a position where he needs to sell and has already taken a hit on the agreed price.

Possible solution #1

Seller may be in a position to remedy a portion of the work, or the most immediate work, at his expense, if the buyer commits to go ahead with the purchase.

Possible solution #2

Buyer agrees to proceed with the purchase and carry out the works due, but only if he receives a discount equivalent to a certain percentage of the cost of remedial work.

Below are examples of some real attempts of buyers to deal with the fallout of a structural survey. As can be seen, the outcome was different in each case.

Example 1 – Waterford

A purchaser looking for a residential site to build on runs into difficulty with local planning restrictions. As an alternative, he selects an unoccupied house on a suitable site that offers potential to build a new home. The house is negotiated well below market value on the basis that it is suitable as a site only – that is, not for use as a home in its present condition.

Unsurprisingly, the structural survey reveals many issues. The buyer re-negotiates aggressively, on foot of the survey, to achieve a further level of discount.

Result: The discount is sought inappropriately using plunder tactics – the relationship with the seller completely breaks down as no goodwill remained and the deal fell through.

Example 2 – South Dublin

Sale agreed for a 1970s four bedroom dormer, subject to structural survey. The survey shows up minor issues, such as poor insulation and poor ventilation. Overall, the condition was consistent with the age of the property. The seller in this case could be classed as motivated. He tries to problem-solve and generously agrees to make minor repairs, at his own expense.

Result: The buyers were a young couple and very concerned about the report. They panic unnecessarily and withdraw before taking any time to understand the findings.

Example 3 – Kildare

A three bedroom semi-detached in a good location, sourced off-market and below market value. The structural survey reveals that the windows do not comply with current building regulations and that there are other minor issues.

Result: Re-negotiation is unsuccessful due to the massively discounted price, but the buyer knew that the house was a bargain, even with the additional cost of new windows, so he chooses to proceed with the purchase.

KEY POINTS FROM CHAPTER 18

- ❖ On foot of the structural survey, the buyer may need or want to re-negotiate the agreed purchase price.
- ❖ This should only be done where there is a structural issue of genuine concern.
- ❖ This is phase three of negotiations, but in reality it is about problem-solving and it is likely the buyer and seller will be able to work together for mutual benefit.
- ❖ These negotiations may be dealt with by the buyer or his solicitor with the estate agent or the vendor's solicitor.
- ❖ Negotiations are based upon the list of necessary works required together with projected costs that the buyer presents to the seller.
- ❖ The negotiations here are more complex as both parties have invested time, energy and money in each other by this point in the process.

Chapter 19

PROCEDURE AT AUCTION

The new reality for Irish buyers

A property auction is best described as a process that allows interested parties to make competitive bids, which establishes the current market value of the property *at that time* in an open, transparent and public forum. Auction rooms in Ireland have long been considered the domain of seasoned investors, developers and farmers. In the past, home-buyers rarely made an appearance and, for first-time buyers, this was not really an option. But that was in the past. The housing market has changed beyond all recognition over the past five years. The buyers dominating the residential market are home-buyers. These buyers have a need for housing, are choosing to purchase but, having escaped the wrath of the property crash by grace and timing, will only be encouraged to enter or re-enter the market when it is safe to do so. They need assurances, and these assurances are unlikely to come from government or media. These buyers need to be sure they are not paying more than the property is worth. As discussed in the earlier chapter on valuations, market value is always difficult to ascertain but never more than now. Public auction, by its very nature, is the truest measure of *a lot* (as each property at auction is referred to) or a property's so-called market value on a particular day. In fact, it could be said that, in the current uncertain market with the prolonged delay in introducing the National Property Price Register, public auction is the only verifiable measure of real market value. However, poor demand on the day can drive down the price and, by extension, the value of a specific property resulting in below market value (BMV) deals for the lucky bidder. In many instances, poor performance at auction is less about the property and more about the lack of strategic marketing in advance by the auctioneer and a failure to attract the right buyers.

The best working example of this was seen in 2010 when a leading auctioneering group in Ireland held a large auction, where residential lots suitable for home-buyers dominated the line-up; however, few home-buyers turned up. Those who did attend on the day were unprepared, in terms of research. Cash investors, who attended in expectation of a stock of discounted properties, were disappointed. There were no loss leaders or sacrificial cows that day. By way of comparison, just months later, a local authority held an auction to dispose of several residences that had been acquired by way of compulsory purchase order (CPO) in previous years. The homes were compromised by their location – in close proximity to a national motorway and had not been occupied for several years at that stage. The local authority had done its homework. It knew that what type of buyer was required for each building and marketed accordingly. The advised minimum values (AMVs) were enticing and just one of the five lots failed to attract any bids. Properties that sold on the day were properties that the eventual owners had researched and pursued. Property auctions are much less about chance than buyers realise; they are about preparation in advance and strategy on the day.

Auctions dominated the Irish property market in 2011. Looking forward into 2012 and 2013, auctions are going to play an even greater role in the marketplace and home-buyers will need to deal with them. This is likely to happen for a number of reasons, namely:

- Sellers are motivated to select the sale through public auction route where they are unconvinced by the estate agent's valuation.

- Buyers are no longer willing to accept the lack of transparency or distorted valuations; they need assurances of value.

- The sheer stock of available properties makes marketing or promotion an issue for sellers and their estate agents. Public auctions in the past repelled home-buyers but, in the present climate, will attract them.

- Banks and mortgage companies are sitting on large stocks of repossessed houses and apartments for the last five years. Several have already held large scale auctions with many more announced for 2012 already. This trend is set to continue.

- NAMA, under its *Code of Practice*, provides for the sale of assets by way of public auction or competitive tendering.

In practice, properties listed for auction are advertised at least three weeks in advance of the auction date. Open viewings and/or viewings by appointment will take place during that period. From the start, buyers will be made aware of the AMV of the property. This is the stated valuation of the property and is not subject to change in the three week marketing period prior to auction.

Buyers must not confuse the AMV with the reserve price, which is the minimum price that a seller will accept on the day through the auction process. Under the standard *Law Society Conditions of Sale*, all auctions have a reserve price, unless specifically stated. The reserve price generally is determined in the lead up to or on the day of the auction by the seller and may or may not be communicated to potential buyers, depending on the strategy employed by the seller. Most private sellers do not disclose the reserve price; however, bank properties sometimes state the reserve price in order to encourage buyers who need encouraging to engage with the auction process. Where the reserve price is stated, the highest offer that matches or exceeds that price will secure the property. The UK multi-lot auction concept of 'maximum reserve' pricing was introduced to Ireland in 2011 and is discussed later in this chapter.

Advantages & Disadvantages of Buying at Auction

There are many advantages for buyers to buying at auction, principally:

- The prepared buyer has access to BMV properties that would be difficult to pinpoint in a search of online sellers' websites.

- It is much easier to spot the signs of a motivated seller at auction and buyers may even be made aware of a seller's circumstances prior to auction.

- Auctions grant inexperienced buyers access to distressed or impaired assets directly from the bank. This is a new development for the residential market in Ireland but one that is likely to gain ground in the coming years.

- Auctions are the most reliable way to establish market value, in the absence of a National Property Price Register, particularly in the current uncertain market.

- Auctions provide much needed transparency on property prices achieved, which is crucial for the Irish market, as they are the most reliable source of data after mortgage reporting. While the volume of auctioned properties traditionally has been relatively low, this increased hugely in 2011 and this trend will certainly continue.

- Where a property fails to attract bids at auction or fails to achieve the seller's reserve price, buyers have a great opportunity to secure a bargain post-auction. By then, the seller should have revised the reserve price based on failure of the property to sell.

The rules surrounding property auctions and the terms and conditions of sale are very pro-buyer and, by extension, anti-buyer.

There are disadvantages for buyers and pitfalls that they need to be aware of, namely:

- The AMV might well be strategic. That is to say, a low AMV might not be indicative of market value but rather used to attract interest in the property. In the local authority auction, discussed earlier, one home had an AMV of €230,000 but actually achieved a price of €345,000, 50 per cent in excess of the guide price. This is particularly frustrating for buyers who have wasted time and money researching the property, having it surveyed and having the legal title examined by their solicitor. A low AMV also will increase the competition levels for bargain-hunters.

- Massive amounts of preparation go into a finding and researching a property. This requires effort on the part of the buyer with no assurances of securing the property on the day. It is a risk but one worth taking as, if the buyer is successful, he will have acquired the right property and can feel confident about the market value.

- As any pundit will know, buying property is subject to risk – always. What varies is the level of risk and how the buyer protects against it. Buying property through auction presents a higher level of risk for buyers. That risk may be minimised but not excluded altogether – for example, despite having approval in principle (AIP), the buyer might be denied a mortgage.

- The bidding is unconditional; it cannot be made dependent upon the sale of an existing home or subject to mortgage. For this reason, it is absolutely essential to prepare fully and thoroughly prior to the auction.

- Where a bid is successful, the buyer is obliged to proceed with the purchase. The contracts for sale are signed on the day of the auction and the legal deposit handed over, usually 10 per cent of the agreed price. There is no equivalent of a 'cooling-off period' that buyers of a washing machine on credit might be afforded. Failure to complete the purchase will result in a forfeiture of the deposit and potentially litigation for breach of contract. In contrast, the seller has a legal right to withdraw at any stage in the process before hammer falls.

- Finally, the greatest pitfall for *unprepared* buyers is that they might be successful in their bid and secure the property but not be in a position to complete the transaction within the prescribed period of 28 days. If this happens, the buyers should consult with their solicitor as soon as possible.

Auction Preparation

Traditional advice or commentary on property auctions generally advises inexperienced buyers to avoid them; however, home-buyers in the current market cannot afford to step back from this challenge. With the likelihood of more high-volume bank auctions and more motivated sellers in the marketplace, together with difficulties in ascertaining market value, auctions are going to play a much greater role in the passing of property. The good news for inexperienced buyers is that very few bargains are achieved in the auction room itself; invariably, they are achieved as a direct result of the preparation in advance. In Chapter 4, the concept of a personal property team was discussed. When competing with other buyers at auction, the benefits of having a good working relation with a relevant team of property professionals are many.

There are a significant number of steps that must be undertaken and checks that should be carried out before the auction, most notably:

1. Buyers should attend the auction of any properties similar to what they are seeking. There is no point attending an auction for agricultural land if a three bedroom semi is required. This will educate the buyers on the practice of auctions in Ireland. It

is worthwhile to watch skilled bidders in action when there is no pressure to get involved. Alternatively, buyers may attend auction training sessions with a reputable buyers' firm, experienced in the Irish auction scene.

2. Buyers should view the property thoroughly, as discussed in Chapter 14, on at least one occasion to ensure that it is the right property for them and to carry out a cursory inspection. As there is no pre-negotiation possible for auction properties, buyers will need to ask questions of the auctioneer, listen carefully to the responses and build up a picture of the seller and /or their circumstances.

3. Research should be carried out on the immediate and surrounding areas to help buyers ascertain the true value of the property, having regard to the local demand and supply or over-supply as the case may be.

4. Buyers who intend to finance their purchase by way of a mortgage must consult with their lender in advance and let them know about the auction and the property being pursued. It is a good idea to have obtained written approval in principle in advance of attending the auction.

5. Buyers are advised to have the property surveyed by a qualified engineer or building surveyor. The surveyor will check that no development has taken place on the property that requires planning permission without that said permission having been obtained. The surveyor also might be in a position to check for any planned developments in the area that may impact on the value of the property. If not, the buyer should investigate the *Local Area Plan* through the county council.

6. The next step is for the buyer to obtain a copy of the draft contract for sale, together with the copy title deeds and supporting documentation, from the seller's solicitor and have their own solicitor inspect same. One word of caution, where the contracts and title are not made available until a few days before the auction, this may be strategic and a particularly

thorough inspection is advised. Tip: The solicitor might be in a position to find out how many sets of contracts were issued; this will help the buyer to assess in advance the likely competition from other buyers.

7. The final task before the big day is for buyers to set their ideal price and maximum limit for acquiring the property in question. The ideal price is what the buyers ideally would offer to secure the property, if it was not subject to auction. The limit figure is not necessarily the maximum mortgage approval or maximum budget but rather the most the property is worth *to the buyer*. This figure is reached having due regard to the research findings, demand or competition in the room, the buyer's budget, costs to upgrade or finish the property and, most importantly, having regard to the ascertainable market value. No buyer can afford to pay more than the property is worth. Tread carefully and do not treat the limit as a target.

At the Traditional Land or Single House Auction

Buyers have two options when it comes to bidding at auction. They can bid themselves or engage a specialist buyers' broker to attend and bid on their behalf. There are a number of advantages to outsourcing this function to a professional; they bring experience and the weight of reputation to the proceedings (this should never be underestimated – Ireland is a very small country). Also, the professional is well-briefed with the buyer's instructions in advance so there is no risk of ego-driven bidding or getting carried away as buyers so often do in an auction scenario. Buyers who choose to bid themselves should have someone with them to monitor the behaviour, demeanour and bids of competing buyers. This 'wing man' also should keep the buyer in check when/if the bidding heats up. Where buyers are planning to bid themselves, they really ought to have attended another auction in advance to familiarise themselves with how it works in reality.

Unlike major, multi-lot bank or distressed property auctions, traditional land or one-off house auctions in Ireland are something of a spectator sport and attendance of 30 to 50 people is entirely normal. Buyers should not be intimidated by this; a crowd of 50 attendees rarely will produce more than three or four bidders but the crowd does add to the ambience of the event. Auctions usually take place in a room at the auctioneer's office or in a local hotel, if a large crowd is expected. It is usually more advantageous for an intending bidder to sit or stand to the rear of the room or hall but bidders should ensure that they are within sight of the auctioneer. Most auctioneers will have one or two colleagues beside them watching for any bids that they miss. It is worth noting here that it is the bidders' responsibility to make themselves seen and heard by the auctioneer.

Before the auction kicks off, the seller's solicitor will read through the essentials of the title and through the special conditions of sale attaching to the property. They will deal with any queries on title at this stage but buyers should be aware that this is merely a formality to comply with the rules for auctions. No intending bidder should be hearing about the title for the first time five minutes before bidding starts. While the bidding process may vary from one auction to another, they tend to follow the same pattern. Anyone who has attended auctions previously will be aware that bidding is usually slow to get started. The auctioneer must coax the first bidder and this can take about 5 to 10 minutes (this does not apply to bank auctions, which are discussed later). To the uninitiated, there appears to be little interest in the property. Buyers should not be fooled though; silence at this stage is strategic. This is also a vulnerable point for buyers. By engaging too early or too vehemently, they are showing their hand. Remember, the key is to find a motivated seller at auction, not to become a motivated buyer! While every auctioneer will deny the practice of what is commonly referred to as dummy bids or 'taking bids from the wall', anecdotally, it used to be very prevalent. It would be naïve not to acknowledge its existence at this stage and buyers are urged to be observant and pay attention to other bidders – in particular, to the first bidder.

When it comes time for the bidding, there are several different strategies that can be used, depending upon the value of the property, the number of competing bidders and how much is known about the seller and their circumstances. In most instances, it is sensible to hold back and watch the bidding evolve. If there are two or more bidders, it is not necessary to engage. Let the bidders fight it out until there is only a single bidder left. If, at this stage, the price is in excess of the buyer's limit, the buyer should not get involved. If the price is still within range, there is only one other buyer to contend with and this is when the buyer should start.

As the bidding continues, it is easy for buyers to lose control. If this happens, it is important to slow things down. Do not make another bid until absolutely necessary. When it proves necessary to make a further bid to stop another buyer securing the property, alter the value of increase – for example, if successive bids have each increased by €5,000, bid with an increase of €1,000. The auctioneer may refuse to accept this level of increase but it is a risky decision for him to take as he may lose the bidder.

Almost every property will have a reserve price – the lowest price that the seller is willing to accept. Private owners rarely disclose their reserve so, in most cases, buyers will not be aware of it unless and until the auctioneer announces that the reserve has been reached and the owner is happy to sell. (In reality, the reserve price may have been reached many bids ago.) This is only ever done if there is more than one bidder. After this point, the remaining bidders continue with the bidding until there is only one remaining. The highest bidder secures the property.

If there is only one bidder but the reserve has not been reached (or sometimes even where the reserve has been reached), the property is withdrawn from the auction and the highest bidder is invited to post-auction negotiations with the seller. This is perhaps the single, most unfair auctioneering practice. It completely defies the very concept of auction and buyers are advised that they can decline to enter these talks. In fact, in a bid to stamp out this unfair practice, every bidder is encouraged to let the auctioneer know in advance that they are bidding at auction only and will not retire into private negotiations. With this communicated, sellers will have the choice either to accept the highest bid or to withdraw the property and try to sell it through private treaty. This point cannot be made strongly enough. The auction process is pro-seller; buyers should not perpetuate this further by handing over their only advantage. Simply put, if the property is put to public auction and achieves the reserve, it should sell at public auction – too much property business has taken place behind closed doors; buyers need to assert themselves here to stamp out this practice for once and for all.

2011: A Year of Auction Firsts for Ireland

Several Irish auctioneering firms tried to stimulate the market by hosting multi-lot auctions of their most saleable properties, offered by their most motivated sellers. There was an expectation of low prices. Unfortunately, the prices did not prove low enough. In fact, it was not until UK auctioneering giants, Allsop, partnering with Dublin new-comers, Space Property Consultants, burst onto the Irish market, with a whole new set of auction 'rules', that buyers began to emerge. Throughout 2011, that alliance held four multi-lot auctions, and sold an amazing 92 per cent of all properties offered.

It is fair to say that the entrance of Allsop into the Irish market changed the face of auctions in Ireland. Allsop introduced the concept of a stated 'maximum reserve price', rather than using the traditional AMV. Maximum reserve price means that, once bidding has reached the stated maximum reserve, the highest competing bid thereafter will secure the property. As this figure is the maximum, in reality, the sellers may accept less on the day. This is a much more favourable system for buyers but had yet to be adopted by the majority of Irish auctioneers. One firm that did adopt this pricing model for their multi-lot auction is Merlin, the homegrown experts in the car auction business. Merlin entered the property market in late 2011 and experienced a slow start in 2012; however, it is expected to offer properties aimed at home-buyers and should prove to be contenders in this space. It also is expected that NAMA will need to hold a large scale residential auction at some point, most likely in late 2012 or early 2013, and it is appropriate that this should be done through one of Ireland's nationwide estate agencies.

These new auctions are on a much larger scale in terms of the actual number of lots offered, but also in terms of bidders in attendance. It is not unusual now to see hundreds of people turning up to large venues to watch in excess of 100 properties go under the hammer. Buyers who are intending to bid should bring with them two forms of valid identification and a cheque/draft. In instances where the venues are filled to capacity, entrance may be restricted to bidders only, no spectators, and proof of funds will be used to determine this.

Bidding at these auctions is very different. It is hectic, aggressive and fast-paced. Properties sell within an average of just over three minutes each. It is unlikely that a bidder will be able to watch other bidders through the crowd so it is always recommended to have an ally in the room. This is the reason why many bidders elect to send in a professional, proxy bidder on the day. The auction day can go on for an intense six to eight hours, with only five minute breaks throughout the day. Two-day bank auctions have become popular in the UK, so it is not impossible that the same could happen here in time.

At the moment, these auctions are attracting mainly cash investors, with home-buyers rarely making an appearance; however, since late 2011, lending banks have started to support home-buyers and it is expected that they will have more auction success in the future. Unfortunately, the lead-in time of three weeks, from the date of the catalogue issuing to the auction day, makes it difficult for mortgage lenders to facilitate their buyers.

For this reason, buyers must be exceptionally organised, have finance in place, select their property and contact their mortgage provider at least two weeks in advance of bidding.

Post-auction Considerations

Buyers should pay attention to unsold lots or properties that failed to achieve their reserve because the seller was unrealistic, as they might come within budget in the near future. Also properties that failed to attract a bid at auction may have their guide price revised and present a better opportunity to buyers.

The most common mistake that buyers make throughout the auction process is failing to prepare adequately. Proper preparation can help the buyer to devise a strategy for pricing the property and managing the bidding process to avoid getting swept up in the frenzy of bidding. Do not be put off by an unsuccessful auction or bid; instead buyers should learn from the experience and from the experiences of others in the auction room. After all, no buyer has the time or resources to make all the mistakes themselves!

KEY POINTS FROM CHAPTER 19

- ❖ Auctions are set to become the new reality for residential buyers from 2012.
- ❖ Advantages for the buyer:
  - o Access to BMV properties
  - o Access to more motivated sellers
  - o Establishes market value
  - o Brings transparency to the market.
- ❖ Disadvantages for the buyer:
  - o The AMV pricing may be strategic
  - o There is a huge amount of preparation involved
  - o Bidding is unconditional.

❖ Preparation is the key to success at auction, so buyers must first:

   o Attend other auctions for experience

   o View the property carefully

   o Have the property surveyed

   o Have the legal title checked by a solicitor.

❖ Unsuccessful bidders should not 'retire into talks' with the auctioneer, post-auction. Auctioneers need to learn that bidding at auction is how the market speaks. They can no longer ignore the market. They must listen to it, and respect it. The highest bid constitutes current market value and buyers are urged not to pay a cent more in private post-auction negotiation than they would in the auction room, otherwise they are effectively bidding against themselves.

❖ The most current source of all multi-lot auctions is the Buyers' Broker Ltd. blog, which may be found at **www.buyersbroker.ie/blog**. This blog contains details of all forthcoming auctions, properties going under the hammer, result prices and relevant commentary from the auction room.

Chapter 20

CONSIDERATIONS FOR RESIDENTIAL INVESTORS

How to compete for limited finance

Until recently, residential investment property was considered to be a highly tax-efficient and low-risk method of investing for the future. Mid-year 2006 reports indicated that the growth in property prices and rental income were beginning to slow down, but that did not trigger major alarm bells to investors at the time. In the decade leading up to 2006, property prices had increased by between 260 and 400 per cent, and it was generally accepted that this was unsustainable. Most speculators anticipated a downturn in the market at some stage; a fall in property values of 10 to 15 per cent was forecasted. Given the massive gains made in the previous 10 years, this was referred to simply as a 'market correction'. No single market commentator foresaw the sheer scale of the crash, the depth of the recession, the global nature of the credit crunch or the level of ineptitude within the Irish banking sector that, in time, surely will be likened to a comedy of errors.

For residential investors, the huge stocks of rental property that flooded the market could not be supported by demand in any areas. Figures collected from the property sales and rentals website daft.ie suggest that homes to let hit an all-time high of approximately 23,400 in mid-2009, from a reasonable 6,200 in 2007. This led to a drop in rents achieved and prolonged periods of vacancy, effectively devastating the portfolios of many investors. The situation is now stabilising to a degree, with current data suggesting a total number of units to let of 18,000. It is important to note that, while pockets of over-supply still exist in areas of low population or high unemployment, rents in the capital actually rose slightly throughout 2010 and 2011. This means that the all-important yields have improved. The average range is now 5 to 6 per cent, though as an investment class that is risky in the short term. A yield percentage of less than the APR, or the cost of borrowings, should only ever be considered when the likelihood of capital appreciation is strong. Between 5 and 8 per cent was achieved by savvy investors in the Tiger years, so there is no reason why investors should accept anything less now – the key lies in sourcing the right property at the right price.

Mortgaged residential investors are not expected to play a big role in the market in 2012/2013. This is due, in large part, to financing difficulties. Where once buy-to-let mortgages were the bread-and-butter of Irish lenders, this credit has effectively dried up and investors will find it tough to put through even the best deals. This is particularly frustrating for those who can see the opportunities that this phase of the market offers, but are unable to access funds. Arguably, this is the best time in over a decade to invest in property, though that may only be possible if the investor is sitting on significant cash reserves. Any investor considering re-entering the property market over the next year or two should be prepared to take a long-term view of the investment and have the resources to deal with a prolonged slump or delayed recovery in the market.

Sourcing a Deal

Sourcing a good investment deal is very different from sourcing property, as discussed in Chapter 8. Most experienced buyers will know that a cheap property can be acquired cheaply in any market conditions; the skill for investors is to acquire a quality property cheaply. There is no magic shortcut to this; deals are generally created, not found ready-packaged on property sales websites.

When it comes to sourcing a good investment deal, buyers must research areas before identifying one particular location. It is a great feature of the Irish market, unlike in larger countries, that areas can be very clearly defined and categorised. Landlords should know the area they intend to invest in or seek independent advice in terms of property values, rental demand, likely yields, local facilities and levels of industry or employment in the area.

The market can be categorised broadly as follows:

- **Urban – cities and large towns**. Supply is high but demand here is also consistently high among students, professionals and, to a lesser extent, young families. As these areas offer the best hope of employment, even in a recession, vacancy levels here are lower than in more rural areas and offer strong opportunities for investors, but only if the property is acquired at the right price.

- **Suburban – within two to 10 kilometres of urban centres**. Supply here is high and demand remains steady among professionals and young families, but only in the more desirable neighbourhoods. Proximity to transport links, schools, restaurants, etc. will be a big factor in attracting tenants.

- **Commuterville – rural towns, within 50 kilometres' radius of a main urban centre**. Most landlords who bought their first investment property *circa* 2005 probably bought in 'commuterville' – that is, Navan, Carlow, Athy or any stop on the primary routes out of Dublin. The vast majority of these properties were financed by 100+ per cent mortgages and many are in serious negative equity, suffering from low occupancy levels, low rents and low yields. Jobs have been lost with little hope of replacement in the immediate future, so investors looking to buy in these areas should research thoroughly and not be enticed by low prices – there is a reason for those huge price drops.

- **Rural – villages and one-off homes on a private site**. While supply has risen in the most unexpected pockets of rural Ireland, demand has held steady and well-presented country homes are consistently sought after by young families and overseas retirees who find it more tax-efficient to rent. These properties tend to be accidental investments, usually inherited or a one-time family home waiting for the market to recover before being offered for sale. Marital breakdown has increased the supply of rural homes in recent years.

- **Coastal – one time holiday homes**. Year-round demand for coastal homes has decreased and there is a large stock of vacant properties. One particular scheme in the south east, offered for sale by the receivers, failed to attract significant attention despite fire-sale prices. Coastal cottages in habitable condition are currently available below €100,000 due to low demand and lack of funding. As an investment, this one is unlikely to be selected for the yields or growth potential, but for investors looking to secure a bolt-hole by the sea or maybe a future retirement home opportunities abound.

A well thought-out location is still the most likely means to providing substantial returns for investors, with the likely added bonus of capital growth in the long term. The right property is determined by the investor's budget and the type of tenant they wish to attract. Generally, students and professionals will have different expectations of a rental property. Also, it is important to consider whether the area will sustain a growth in property values and whether it would be easy to sell this property in the long term. Residential investment properties may be either houses or apartments, and while apartments are generally smaller and easier to maintain, there is very often an obligation to pay a maintenance charge to a management company. Houses in a suitable location generally will be larger than apartments, and therefore will command a greater rent. However, they also require a greater level of maintenance.

The difference between finding a property and finding a deal is down to the investor's property team – that is, the financial adviser, buyer's broker, letting agent, tax consultant, solicitor and network of other investors. As previously mentioned, a great deal does not tend to be advertised on-line as a ready-to-go proposition but rather created. For instance, a sourcing agent has access to off-market properties, which helps the investor assess the potential in the property without the pressure of competing buyers. A good relationship with the letting agent means that the investor can pick up the phone to enquire about the likely rental situation for a specific property. If the investor moves to secure it, a prompt response from the lender means that offers can be made with confidence. A decisive, finance-ready buyer can make all the difference to a motivated seller. Unconditional contracts and the promise of a prompt closing (no problem for an efficient solicitor) is worth several thousand euro to any motivated seller and the investor can negotiate this benefit. The team in this scenario allows the investor access to below market value (BMV) property and the support to follow through, creating significant savings.

When it comes time to negotiate, which has been covered in three earlier chapters, residential investors are in the best possible position to benefit by *pre-negotiating,* if it is done right. (If the reader has skimmed that chapter, it is definitely worth re-visiting before going any further.) The main reasons for this are: firstly, investors tend to assess properties on paper and are naturally selective about what properties they view; and secondly, because they have no attachment to the property, they will have no difficulty walking away if the seller does not agree to their budget in advance. Not only will this be more effective for identifying motivated sellers, it also will save investors lots of time and shoe leather.

Sourcing Finance

Property is one of the few asset classes that investors can choose to invest in without having the money to finance it, a concept known as leveraging. The majority of a cleverly structured property investment is funded by other peoples' money (OPM), usually from a bank. The principle of the strategy is to use as little of the investor's own cash resources to finance the deal. At the height of the property boom, investors were securing mortgage funding in excess of 110 per cent of the purchase price, which was made possible by acquiring the property below market value. Obviously, these investors are suffering most from negative equity in the current market. Lenders are unlikely to allow that to happen again, at least not until the next generation. The loan to value (LTV) rates have gone way down for residential investors seeking a buy-to-let mortgage.

In the first month of 2011, the Irish mortgage companies open to residential investment mortgage lending, in theory, are as follows: AIB, Bank of Ireland, Ulster Bank, KBC, ICS and IIB. LTVs range from 50 per cent to 80 per cent with variable rates of approximately 4.27 to 4.90. Fixed rates range from 4.50 to 5.94. Anglo Irish Bank (now, the Irish Bank Resolution Corporation Limited – IBRC) and the Irish Nationwide Building Society have closed their doors to all mortgage business.

The various types of mortgages and interest rate options are explained in Chapter 6, 'Sourcing Finance'. Interest-only mortgages are difficult to secure in the current market. Bank of Ireland is one of the few lenders still offering this type of mortgage, and it is offered for a period of three years only, at which time the loan reverts to a standard repayment mortgage.

It is crucial for investors to remember that property investing is a business. As with any other business seeking funding, the investor must prepare a proposal, similar to a business plan for the lender. The onus is very much on the investor to convince the lender that the proposal makes sound, economic sense. The pool of available credit has shrunk to the point where only the very best deals will secure finance. The lenders are cherry-picking mortgage applicants, as is to be expected. Of all the mortgage applications submitted, the best proposal (combination of the person and the property) – that is, a proposal that appears viable to the bank, with a good likelihood of returns – will be successful. When applying for an investment mortgage, it helps to think of it as submitting a proposal for the bank rather than an application. If the investor makes money from the deal, ultimately so too will the bank. All property buyers should remember that banks are commercial in nature; they create an income through lending. They need to lend in order to make money, and the investor needs to borrow in order to make money. Below is a list of details to be included in an investment property proposal.

Property Proposal for Submission to a Lender	
Part 1. About the investor	• Brief biography – areas of expertise • Income • Capital assets • Existing borrowings • Other personal financial details
Part 2. About the property	• Details of the property • Address • Condition • Include photographs • Main selling features
Part 3. About the deal	• Asking price or market value • Likely purchase price • Upgrading required and likely costs • Value to be added • Projected rents – include letting agent advices • Likely capital appreciation • Plans to let or sell in medium term

Property Proposal for Submission to a Lender	
Part 4. Finance required	• Total cost of purchase (include everything) • Amount to be contributed by investor • Amount sought from bank • Terms required to make the investment viable
Part 5. Introduce the team	• Sourcing agent – BMV deal • Financial/taxation advisors • Engineer/Surveyor • Solicitor
Be careful not to work the figures too hard. The lender will see through massaged data, which will damage the integrity of the entire proposal.	

Taxation

Taxation is a huge aspect of property investing and one of the most important considerations for any investor. Residential investors are encouraged to consult with a qualified, professional taxation consultant prior to investing in property. There are several forms of taxation and failure to plan at the start can cause severe problems later that may prove costly to fix. Chapter 5, 'Tax Issues', details the different forms of taxation applicable to all property buyers, and investors should pay particular attention to the property reliefs and exemptions.

To recap, taxes affecting residential investors are:

1. **Stamp duty** – 1 per cent on properties valued up to €1 million, with 2 per cent applying to properties over €1 million.

2. **Capital Gains Tax (CGT)** – A tax on profit or gains that arise on the sale of capital assets at a current rate of 25 per cent.

3. **Capital Acquisitions Tax (CAT)** – A tax on any interest in a real asset acquired by way of a gift or inheritance and is taxable at a current rate of 25 per cent.

4. **Income tax** – Investors must pay tax on received rental income less deductible expenses (listed in Chapter 5). The amount of interest available as a deduction in calculating tax liabilities on rental income was reduced to 75% in 2009.

5. **Non-principal Private Residence tax (NPPR)** – A tax on any residential property not occupied by the owner, €200 *per annum*.

Tax Reliefs and Exemptions

In 1998, extensive reliefs were introduced for investors in an attempt to stimulate investment in less desirable areas in need of regeneration. These schemes were welcomed by investors, but were seen by the general public as tax breaks for high-earners.

The most commonly availed of these schemes were the Section 23 and Section 50 properties, which were used to shelter Irish rental income. Section 23 properties are residential units built in less desirable areas and Section 50 properties are specially-built student accommodation. In general, 75 to 90 per cent of the purchase price qualifies for tax relief as the site element does not qualify. The tax break originally was given as a further deduction against the investor's net rental income, not just from that specific property but from the combined total of all net rental profits within the State in any given year. If the purchaser has significant Irish rental income, the whole of the tax break can be used up in one year. If not, the deductions create a rental loss that is carried forward against the investor's future Irish rental income. The tax relief is clawed back if the property is sold or ceases to be occupied within a period of 10 years from first use.

These so-called section property reliefs have come under pressure in recent times. Major changes were announced in the Budgets 2011 and 2012 as follows:

- Capital allowances claimed on rental properties may only be offset against rental income from the specific property concerned.

- In the case of seven and 10-year schemes, any unused capital allowances may not be carried forward beyond the seven or 10 year write-off period for the property concerned.

- In the case of schemes where the capital allowances are claimed over a period exceeding 10 years but less than 25 years, the write off period is reduced to seven years and any unused allowances may not be carried forward beyond the seven-year write-off period.

- Section 23 relief may only be offset against rental income from the property in relation to which the relief is being claimed.

- Any remaining Section 23 relief will be lost at the end of the 10-year holding period.

- If a Section 23 property is sold within the holding period, the new owner will not be entitled to claim any Section 23 relief, notwithstanding the claw back suffered by the previous owner.

The *Finance Act 2011* stalled these changes after intense lobbying by various interest groups. The legislative changes are now subject to a commencement order, which investors should monitor as it develops throughout 2012 and 2013. The earliest that the measures may come into effect is 60 days following the publication of an economic impact assessment.

Managing the Property

The key to any business, including the business of property investing, is to create a sustainable income. This means attracting quality tenants, managing the letting and keeping proper records of all income and expenses. Investors can hire an agent to deal with these matters or they can manage the property directly. First-time investors are encouraged to take an active role in dealing with tenant issues.

The rental market is still slow in areas, but landlords can increase their chances of attracting a quality tenant by providing a clean, well-maintained property at a reasonable market rent. Of course, as seasoned landlords will know, lower rent from a reliable, long-term tenant might prove sensible in challenging market conditions. Cash flow is absolutely king for an investor's portfolio. When making financial plans and forecasts, investors should always factor in a void period to allow for weeks between lettings when the property might be empty. Investors are advised to build up some level of a contingency fund to cover expenses to pay for unexpected repairs and maintenance.

Private Residential Tenancies Board

The residential rental market in Ireland is governed by the *Residential Tenancies Act, 2004*, which sets out basic tenancy obligations for landlords and tenants. This Act also established the Private Residential Tenancies Board (PRTB), whose role is to provide dispute resolution for landlords and tenants. It is the body responsible for tenancy registrations; all landlords must register the details of any new tenancies with the board. Landlords should acquaint themselves with their obligations under the *Residential Tenancies Act*: principally to provide a lease, register the tenancy and give adequate notice to tenants in the event that they need to terminate the lease.

The table below details the steps involved in letting property in Ireland.

Letting the Property	
Advertise the vacancy	• Advertise online (daft.ie, myhome.ie etc.) • Use quality photographs • Advertise locally on community boards • List preferences for a tenant.

Letting the Property	
Deal with enquires	• Have a phone checklist ready • Take details of all enquirers • Arrange view times.
Arrange viewings	• Ensure the property is clean and clutter-free • Let current tenants know in advance • Avoid open viewings • Give full information.
Select tenants	• Have a conversation with enquirers • Be objective • Choose the most suitable tenant • Take a holding deposit • Follow-up on references.
Put the lease in place	Download sample form from the PRTB, filling in: • Length of the tenancy • Rent and arrangement to pay • Deposit • Notice periods • Tenant obligations • Special conditions.
Tenant takes occupation	• Meet the tenant to hand over keys • Agree list of contents and condition • Sign the lease agreement • Complete the PRTB Registration form • Collect the deposit and first month's rent • Take the electricity and gas meter readings.
Final checks	• Transfer the utility bills into the tenant's name • Submit the PRTB Registration form • Maintain communication with tenant • Carry out regular inspections of the property.

Investors who are committed to buying in 2012 or 2013 should be realistic about the challenges ahead. There is certainly value to be achieved, particularly through bank auctions and at least one

NAMA auction, but the property needs to be in an area where people choose to live. Where trends are difficult to assess, select an area that is well-serviced by transport links and social facilities, where tenants will have access to employment and their families will have access to quality schools, restaurants and supermarkets.

Here is a little piece of wealth trivia for investors: many US university studies have looked at the world's billionaires and could find no pattern of shared backgrounds, gender or levels of education achieved. The most common denominator was property! The majority made their money through property; and those who did not later invested their acquired billions in property.

KEY POINTS FROM CHAPTER 20

❖ To start, the investors must define the market and then research it. They should not invest until they know the market thoroughly; otherwise they will not recognise BMV opportunities when they arise.

❖ Investor skills lie in buying well. Every deal must be a good deal; do not assume that the property just will appreciate.

❖ Property, like all other markets, goes through cycles. Have reserves in place so that, if a down cycle does take place, the investor has an opportunity to take advantage of bargains.

❖ Investors need to have a two-pronged approach, both a short-term and a long-term strategy: positive cash flow in the short term, with excellent potential for above average appreciation in the long term.

❖ The golden rule: no cheap properties, just quality properties acquired cheaply.

Chapter 21

FOREIGN BUYERS

Selecting the right area and property type

Property in Ireland has always attracted a strong level of demand from overseas buyers, long before the emergence of the Tiger economy at the start of the 21st century. There are many explanations for this, including:

- Irish ties have encouraged expatriates to acquire and keep a base here. In 2009 and 2010, there was a marked increase in cash purchases, and while there is no mechanism for capturing this specific data (Ireland's only accurate data reporting is based on mortgage draw down), it is estimated to have exceeded 15 per cent of market purchases. Anecdotally, a large chunk of these cash buyers were second-generation expatriates looking for a modest home away from home in Ireland. It is generally not expected that these properties would be rented out, but rather used for family purposes. There is certainly an expectation of future capital appreciation on the part of these buyers, despite the poor performance of property currently. Most are buying because they feel now is the right time and they have confidence in the Irish market in the long term.

- Areas of unique scenery have provided the perfect location for holiday homes for buyers of every nationality. The holiday home market in Ireland came to an abrupt halt in 2007 with very few domestic or foreign buyers showing interest; however, 2010 saw the return of foreign buyers, in particular those resident in Germany and the US in search of traditional holiday homes. Areas most in demand were coastal areas in the south east, west and south west of the country, with the midlands faring badly. Budgets are relatively low – few exceed €100,000, which is sufficient to find a traditional cottage within two kilometres of the coast. The oversupply of purpose-built holiday homes on large complexes is failing to hit the right note with these buyers. Those seeking a *pied-à-terre* in the capital might find themselves disappointed by the location and quality of any low value units.

- Favourable tax incentives have encouraged residential and commercial investment from foreign buyers. In particular, 1998 saw the introduction of the Urban Renewal Relief scheme, more commonly known as Section 23 relief (residential properties purchased under this scheme are simply known as Section 23 properties or 'section' properties). Qualifying commercial properties are afforded similar relief. This scheme allows any individual or body to acquire a newly constructed, refurbished or converted residential property situated wholly within a designated area and to offset the rental income against any other rental income arising in Ireland. As mentioned in Chapters 5 and 20, this relief was curtailed in the Budget 2011 but the government failed to give this measure legislative effect in the Finance Act 2011 or 2012.

- Foreign residential investors, particularly those from the UK, seeking capital gains in the medium term have routinely looked to the Irish market. Historically, property in Ireland has doubled in value every seven years, which was greatly accelerated from 2002 to 2006. When compared to the UK property market, which has historically doubled in value every 10 years, it is easy to see why foreign investors favoured these shores. Tiger-era

Ireland offered investors a reasonable yield, usually averaging at 5 per cent, with assumed capital appreciation. Of course, that is no longer the case. Purchase prices have fallen an average of 50 per cent (it varies from 30 to 80 per cent, depending upon the area and property type) and yields are settling around the 5 to 8 per cent mark, but capital appreciation is not expected for several years to come.

- The controversially low corporation tax rate of 12.5 per cent, which entices global industry to Ireland, drives demand in rural cities and towns where foreign companies tends to settle – for example, Kilkenny or Tipperary. The foreign buyer in this instance is usually the company, which acquires properties for two distinct purposes: firstly, to house visiting executives on a short term basis, as an alternative to hotels; and secondly, to house longer-term contract employees, who are subject to short notice relocations. Ireland is coming under increasing Franco-German pressure about the competitiveness of this tax rate and its effect on EU member states.

- Over the past decade, Michael O'Leary, through Ryanair's revolutionary low cost air travel, has made Ireland more accessible than anyone could have believed possible. Our little island is now globally accessible, which has played a huge part in promoting the other factors above. There is a connection between tourism, or critically, a country's status as a desirable holiday destination, and the non-resident property market. This is a strength that Ireland has built up over many decades so it will be interesting to watch how this particular sector of the market performs over the next five years.

Looking forward into 2012 and 2013, Ireland will need to attract overseas buyers back into the market to deal with the unprecedented stock levels nationwide. As a strategy, this is important on two levels: firstly, to increase demand to deal with the volume of over-supply, and secondly, to find buyers for the *type* of properties in over-supply, in other words, apartments. On the first issue, the generally accepted figure for so-called normal supply demands 40,000 new homes per year. As this has dropped to 25,000 for the past two years, and is unlikely to increase for at least another two to three years, the market needs external demand in addition to domestic buyers. To address the second issue, the market needs buyers who will embrace apartment ownership. The Irish culture and psyche has played a huge role in rejecting apartment living, except, of course, for a brief, almost obligatory renting spell in early adulthood. Poor planning design and implementation also has played a part. It is a fair assessment to make about apartments that, outside of areas of high, transient demand in large urban areas, they have not proved very successful with Irish home-buyers and investors will only accept them in limited circumstances – for example, in areas of proven, consistently high yields.

A stock of vacant apartments gradually will be released to the market through NAMA and other lenders in the Irish market so heavy discounts are to be expected. A high level of discount will prove necessary to attract any investors as the yield is still relatively low compared to other countries. Residential yields are unlikely to exceed 6 to 8 per cent. Non-resident investors who approach the Irish market with finance in place will find bargains at this end of the market, as lenders here are unlikely to begin lending to residential investors for another few years. In fact, when they do begin this type of lending again, low-yielding, poorly-located apartment blocks will not attract favour. At least two of the main lenders have closed their doors temporarily to apartment mortgages outside of the main urban centres, and it is unclear how long this embargo on apartments will continue or if other lenders will follow their lead.

With the possibilities of bargains ahead, foreign buyers will need to evaluate the real cost of buying and owning property in Ireland. The following is a list of the likely expenses and outgoings that a non-resident buyer should expect to incur, in addition to the agreed purchase price:

- **Agency fees**. A buyers' broker may provide exclusive representation to buyers and will source, negotiate or acquire property on their behalf. This is covered in greater detail in Chapter 4, 'Building Your Property Team'. Buyers' representatives or property buyers' brokers have become more common in Ireland since 2006. This generally comes as a relief to foreign buyers, particularly those who have already used this type of service to buy property in their own country. The costs here, though varying from one firm to another, are generally between 1 to 2 per cent of the purchase price of the property plus VAT.

- **Stamp duty**. Stamp duty is a form of taxation, imposed upon property buyers by way of a once-off charge, payable at the time of purchase. The stamp duty regime was overhauled in late 2010 and all property buyers will be liable to 1 per cent of the purchase price on residential units up to, but not exceeding, €1 million. Properties in excess of €1 million will attract stamp duty liability of 2 per cent. This generally will be collected by the conveyancing solicitor and submitted on the investor's behalf to the Revenue Commissioners.

- **Legal fees**. Legal fees will vary in accordance with the value of the property and the law firm selected. See Chapter 22 for details.

- **Maintenance**. Maintenance of the property will be a concern for non-resident buyers, and this is particularly true for residential property. Generally, property maintenance encompasses the overall upkeep of a house or apartment and its surrounding gardens. Within apartment blocks, this external upkeep most often is entrusted to the management company (if applicable, management fees will be paid annually per the contract for sale); however, like with houses, property owners will still need to maintain the interiors – that is, painting and decorating, fixing and replacing. If they are absent from the country, they will need to employ an individual or firm to visit the property routinely, mow lawns, clear gutters and carry out other basic tasks to avoid weather damage. Fees start from €450 per year (8 to 12 per cent of rental income), depending on the level and frequency of work required.

- **Letting fees**. If it is the property buyer's intention to rent the property out for all or parts of the year, it is worthwhile making contact with a local letting agent. This agent can advise on value and trends in the current market, promote the property, arrange viewings, vet the tenants, collect rents and deal with tenant issues in the absence of the owner. Lettings fees range from 8 per cent upwards. It is usually more cost-efficient to engage a single firm for letting and maintenance.

- **Taxation**. Taxation is the issue foremost in the minds of non-resident buyers when they investigate the practicalities of the Irish property market. Liability arises under the following categories (for full details see Chapter 5, 'Tax Implications'):

  - NPPR: A tax on non-principal private residences came into effect in 2009, and is currently chargeable at an annual rate of €200.

  - CGT: Capital Gains Tax applies to the profit or gain made on investment or second properties (less deductible expenses) and is chargeable upon sale of the property at the current rate of 25 per cent.

o CAT: Where Irish property is passed to another person
   by way of an inheritance or a gift, Capital Acquisitions
   Tax is chargeable at the current rate of 25 per cent
   (thresholds apply).

o VAT: Value-added tax may be chargeable on newly-
   built, residential Irish property. If applicable, it is
   chargeable at the rate of 13.5% of the value of the
   property.

o Income tax: Non-resident landlords must register with
   the Revenue Commissioners for Income Tax within
   the State (Form TR1) and they are assessed for tax
   based upon rental profits (rent received less allowable
   expenses), and a further deduction or credit will be
   made for the tax already submitted directly by the
   tenant (20 per cent of gross rental income). The tenant
   supplies the landlord with a Form 185 to show that the
   20 per cent has been accounted for by Revenue.

Non-resident buyers who intend to finance the purchase through
an Irish lender also should factor in the cost of borrowings and
mandatory insurance, as detailed in Chapter 6, 'Securing Finance'.

Other Considerations

Non-resident property owners are advised to consult with a
solicitor about drafting a will to ensure that the property can be
fully dealt with in the event of death. Irrespective of the owner's
country of residence, in the absence of a valid, properly-drafted
will, Irish intestacy laws will determine how any property situated
in Ireland will be dealt with.

Overseas buyers are subject to the same money laundering
requirements as Irish buyers – that is, they are obliged to provide
evidence of their identity and residence. Original documents will
be copied and the copies retained by the estate agent for a period
of five years. It is worth noting here that, if the estate agent has

reason to suspect money laundering, they are obliged to report their suspicions to the relevant authorities.

KEY POINTS FROM CHAPTER 21

❖ Ireland attracts consistently strong levels of demand from overseas buyers; while this has eased in recent years, there is still a market there.

❖ Costs incurred are most likely:

  o Stamp duty

  o Agency and legal fees

  o Maintenance.

❖ Tax liabilities include:

  o Non Principal Private Residence Tax (NPPR)

  o Capital Gains Tax (CGT)

  o Capital Acquisitions Tax (CAT)

  o Value-added Tax (VAT)

  o Income tax on rents received.

❖ In the absence of a valid, properly-drafted will, Irish intestacy laws will determine how any property situated in Ireland will be dealt with.

Chapter 22

THE LEGAL PROCESS

How to work efficiently with your solicitor

Engaging a Solicitor

Any buyer who finances their purchase by way of a mortgage is required to engage the services of a member of the Law Society of Ireland, a solicitor, to deal with the conveyancing. This is the term used to describe the legal process between two parties whereby property is bought, sold, transferred or re-mortgaged.

For first-time buyers in particular, this may be the first time that they have had to engage a solicitor on their behalf. The temptation is usually to hire either their parents' family solicitor or the cheapest online service they can find. Neither is a great strategy. The conveyancing solicitor, when engaged, will become part of the buyers' property team, so it is important to do a little shopping around. Find a firm that has the expertise and professionalism that will be necessary to carry out the work while maintaining a high level of customer service. Buying property, especially a home, is stressful for a myriad of reasons. Any professional who is a member of the buyers' property team must improve the experience, not add to the stress. Unanswered telephone calls and messages, when the buyer genuinely needs advice or a response, are guaranteed to not only add to, but actually create, stress. Reputation means a lot, but personal referrals are more reliable. Speak to other buyers; ask friends who have bought property recently which firm they used and how they would rate the service. There is an online resource that allows users to rate their experience with any particular law firm;

however, by way of caution, this tends to be vexatious in nature so its merit is questionable. Researching a few firms online, browsing their websites and checking out their social media contributions generally will tell a lot about them.

Buyers may choose between a specialist conveyancing service and a general practice law firm that deals with conveyancing but not exclusively. The advantages of dealing with a specialist service are many. Experience and finely-honed skills are to be expected. Another advantage is that many conveyancing solicitors at this stage are using technology such as online file view, email and SMS notification systems that will keep the buyer updated regularly throughout the process. Online file view is a great facility for watchful buyers as the entire conveyancing process may be accessed on a dedicated website. This type of communication is efficient, but buyers may find it lacking in terms of building a relationship of trust and confidence with their solicitor.

Buyers using the services of a property buyers' broker will have been represented throughout the sourcing and negotiations phase; however, for all other buyers, this will be the first element of professional representation so it is important to be clear about the solicitor's function. The solicitor is not there to negotiate or comment on the deal that has already been agreed between the buyer and seller. The solicitor's role is to record this deal or agreement to buy, to hand over security to the bank and to register the new home-owner's interest with the Property Registration Authority (PRA).

As with any service-user and service-provider dynamic, the buyer has a responsibility to manage the solicitor and their relationship. Knowledge of the legal process, and of the solicitor's role within that process, will enable the buyer to work more effectively with the solicitor to ensure that both are pulling together rather than against each other. Simple tips for buyers are to:

1. Engage the solicitor as early in the transaction as possible.

2. Deal with all correspondence and return all calls as promptly as possible.

3. Provide the solicitor with all required information promptly.

4. Attend to sign paperwork as soon as an appointment may be made.

5. Understand that, where the solicitor has an assistant, the assistant will be in a position to answer certain questions and pass on any information to the solicitor, which cuts down on unnecessary phone calls and allows the solicitor to concentrate on the conveyancing.

The Legal Process

Agreement is Reached between Buyer and Seller

The first step of the legal process is when the seller accepts the offer put forward by the buyer to purchase the property in question. The buyer then pays a booking deposit, generally €5,000 though it can vary in accordance with the value of the property. The booking deposit should not be confused with the legal contact deposit, which is payable upon signing of contracts for sale. The booking deposit alone has no legal effect and is fully refundable in the event of the buyer or seller deciding not to proceed. In a buyer's market, this may leave the seller feeling vulnerable until such time as contracts have been completed, and the converse is also true. A sales letter is furnished by the auctioneer to both party's solicitors, which sets out the agreed sales terms and conditions.

Contracts for Sale are Issued

Contracts for sale are issued in duplicate by the seller's solicitor to the buyer's solicitor, together with copies of any supporting title documentation. Upon examination of the contract and title documents, the buyer's solicitor may raise pre-contract enquiries, in the form of requests for clarification or for further information or documentation.

Signing of Contracts for Sale
When the buyer's solicitor is satisfied that the title is in order and
the mortgage documentation issues from the lender, the buyer will
then meet with their solicitor to complete the mortgage papers and
contracts for sale in duplicate. The legal deposit – generally the
balance of 8 or 10 per cent, depending upon the mortgage LTV – is
payable at this stage. Contracts and monies are returned to the
seller's solicitor with a specified closing date, usually within a
period of four to six weeks. If the property in question is a second-
hand home, a draft purchase deed accompanies the contract for
approval by the seller's solicitor.

Seller Now Completes the Contract
The seller attends his solicitor's office to sign the contracts for sale
in duplicate. One original contract is retained in that office and the
second contract is returned to the buyer's solicitor. At this stage,
the contracts are considered to be legally binding. Contracts were
exchanged and signed by both parties, as well as a deposit having
been paid in full.

Cheque Requisition
The buyer's loan cheque is now requested from the mortgage
company in advance of the contractual closing date. As this can
take a week or up to 10 days to issue, it is important that any
outstanding issues with the lender are complied with at least two
weeks in advance. Buyers should double-check this directly with
their lender or mortgage broker.

Closing
On the day of closing, the buyer's solicitor must carry out searches
against the property to ensure that no changes have taken effect
between the time of examination of title and the closing date that
would affect either the buyer or the bank's interest over the
property. Once those searches are clear, the balance of funds will
be transferred to the seller and keys will be handed over to the
buyer. Upon closing, ownership of the property transfers and the

buyer is now the owner of the property. There was a time when closings took place in the solicitor's office with a sense of occasion; now, it is more common to close the transaction by post.

Registration

While the new home-owner is celebrating their move, the solicitor will still be on duty as the transfer deed must be lodged with the Revenue Commissioners within a period of 30 days. Once stamped by Revenue, this deed must be submitted to the Property Registration Authority so that the buyer is legally registered as the new owner. Once the registration is completed, the buyer's solicitor must send the title deeds to the mortgage company as security for the loan. In the instance of a cash buyer, the deeds are returned to the owners or retained by the solicitor for safekeeping.

Legal Fees

Legal fees generally will vary in accordance with the value of the property and the law firm selected. Fixed price conveyancing services, which effectively reduced the scale of professional fees from 1 per cent to a flat rate of €750, were introduced in 2001. Professional fees of €1,000 to €1,500 are quite typical for a property below €500,000. VAT is charged on the professional fee at a rate of 23 per cent, together with expenses. Buyers are advised to shop around and not to be influenced by price alone – look for genuine client testimonials.

Legal Expenses and Outlays

The figure for expenses refers to payments made by the solicitor, on behalf of the buyer, for example, required searches and property registration fees. This figure should not vary significantly from one firm to another. Some may apply a nominal charge for telephone and postage of approximately €130.

Property Registration Authority Fees

A registration fee will be payable to the PRA in respect of the new ownership and mortgage after the purchase has been completed and the deed of transfer has been stamped by the Revenue Commissioners.

The PRA comprises the two different systems of registration in Ireland: the Land Registry and the Registry of Deeds. In general, agricultural land is most likely to be registered title. Most urban properties, and in particular older properties, generally will be what is referred to as unregistered title. One of the main differences between the two is that, with the registered title, one essentially is dealing with one document of title – namely, the land certificate. The buyer's solicitor does not have to look behind the land certificate to trace the previous owners. With an unregistered title, a vendor's solicitor offers a number of documents of title, tracing back the ownership of the particular property for up to 40 years so that a chain of ownership is disclosed and the buyer's solicitor may be satisfied as to its completeness.

The Land Registry fees payable on the property depend on the value of the property and are as follows:

Land Registry Fees	
Registration of mortgage	€126.97
Registration of Ownership (value thresholds)	
Not in excess of €10,000	€126.97
In excess of €10,000 but not in excess of €20,000	€190.46
In excess of €20,000 but not in excess of €40,000	€253.95
In excess of €40,000 but not in excess of €200,000	€380.92
In excess of €200,000 but not in excess of €300,000	€507.90
In excess of €300,000	€634.87

Other Charges	
Land Certificate	€25.39
Certificate of Charge	€6.35
Copy Folio	€25.39

For properties registered in the Registry of Deeds, the following registration fees will apply:

Registry of Deeds Fees	
Memorial of Mortgage	€44.44
Counterpart of Mortgage	€12.70
Memorial of Conveyance/ Assignment	€44.44
Counterpart of Memorial of Conveyance/Assignment	€1270

Other Outlays

Other out-of-pocket expenses that the conveyancing solicitor is likely to incur are professional search fees. These searches are mandatory and must be carried out on the day of closing to ensure that there are no charges attaching to the property. In essence, they update aspects of the title and supporting documentation that the solicitor already has examined prior to the buyer signing contacts. Search fees range from €120 to €240, depending on the property.

Commissioner for Oaths' fees also will be incurred to the approximate value of €20. Once again, this is a mandatory requirement as certain declarations and affidavits must be completed in the presence of a Commissioner for Oaths for validity.

Title Insurance

This insurance deals with the legal title to property, rather than the property itself. Unlike other forms of insurance that insure the current homeowner against things that may happen in the future, title insurance protects against matters that happened in the past. Since the introduction of title insurance to Ireland in 1998, it has been used exclusively to date for re-mortgages rather than purchase of property. It protects the homeowner from any loss resulting from title defects, fraud and forgery related to the title of the property. This is not a substitute for the conveyancing process above; however, it does provide existing homeowners with a low-cost alternative on the following instances:

- Remortgage of any residential property
- Consolidating debts
- Releasing home equity
- Switching lenders for a better interest rate
- Transferring property into joint names.

It works by replacing the standard solicitor's undertaking and certificate of title with the insurance certificate. The homeowner still will need to consult with their solicitor.

The advantages of using title insurance are significantly lower fees, starting from €150 plus VAT, and a much shorter process time. The traditional approach to remortgages would result in a loan cheque taking six to eight weeks to issue. Using this method can reduce that time to two to three weeks.

New Legislation Relating to Multi-unit Developments

The new multi-unit developments (MUD) legislation was enacted in April 2011 by the Department of Justice & Law Reform. This legislation was called for by industry professionals and home-owners alike, and it is expected to promote apartment living among Irish buyers who have tended to favour houses. It is very timely, considering the stock of available apartments, which is disproportionately higher than the stock of houses nationwide. The MUD legislation will improve the rights of apartment owners, and aims to stop the developers of a particular complex from abusing their power by defining the rights and obligations of those in control of the management companies. It sets out what services and offerings can be charged for, and how those charges are to be calculated. Furthermore, it obliges the management company to hold annual meetings where existing apartment owners may get involved with the budget and their vote will influence the future application of the management company funds.

Obligations for Developers under the New Legislation
Developers are now obliged to transfer ownership of the land prior to selling any apartments. The previous obligation was for them to effect the transfer within 30 days of the sale of the last apartment. This was routinely avoided by retaining at least one apartment in every development, referred to by many as the 'pension unit'. Existing developments, those completed or in the course of completion, were due to be handed over before 1 August 2011.

Another change is that developers no longer can have majority shares, weighted shares or any other such biased mechanisms that have the effect of distorting the voting procedure within the management company. This ensures that apartment owners effectively will take over the management of the complex, and the management company simply will be the vehicle for this. Of course, on an equal voting basis, one vote per apartment, developers with a stock of unsold apartments obviously will be in a position to yield more influence than appropriate, so prospective buyers are advised to check this out in advance. While the developer may benefit from increased votes, he also will be subject to equal service charges for each apartment pending sale. The most immediately relevant changes introduced by this legislation is that a qualified majority of 60 per cent of the homeowners can use their vote to remove developers, where that developer has closed down work in the complex and leaves an unfinished site abandoned. In instances where the unfinished estate results in an unsafe environment for apartment owners, the management company (minus the developers) can carry out the necessary repairs and bill the developer for the work.

Obligations of the Management Company under the New Legislation

The management company must produce an annual report, setting out the income received from the apartment owners and details of any expenditure – for example, refuse charges, maintenance and insurance of the communal area, etc. Any assets and liabilities must be declared, together with details of the sinking fund.

The sinking fund refers to that part of the monies collected from apartment owners annually that is put aside to pay for any major renovation or upgrading works that will prove necessary in the future. Essentially, it is a mechanism for spreading the cost of major works over a long period of time so that apartment owners will not face a huge bill when such an event occurs. This is a mandatory requirement for management companies under the new legislation and every apartment owner must contribute to it after the third year of the company's existence. Previously, the required minimum figure was €200 per apartment *per annum*; however, this proviso has now been updated to allow the directors of the management company to make a decision based upon the age and condition of the property and calculate a fair and reasonable sinking fund contribution from that.

This report from the management company also must detail any contacts that the company has with external providers – for example, a maintenance contract and insurance providers. In relation to insurance, this is a big issue for apartment owners and they will want to see details of the premium and the level of cover in this report. The management company is obliged to circulate this report at least 10 days before the annual general meeting

(AGM). Other rules pertaining to the AGM include a provision that meetings must be held close to the apartment complex and all apartment-owners must be given at least 21 days' notice in advance. The voting rights of the apartment-owners will be exercised at the AGM.

One of the most important issues that owners will be called to vote on is the budget. This must be agreed on a majority basis. If, for any reason, the management company finds it necessary to make changes to the agreed budget throughout the year, the apartment owners must be called in to cast a further vote. This measure has been criticised for being micro-management in practice; however, it ensures that no funds are misappropriated or wasted on costly or ineffective services, as happened in the past.

The legislation affords the management company greater powers in relation to the 'Big Brother' manifesto, or the house rules, by allowing the directors to make changes and apply those changes, upon the consent of the majority of apartment-owners. This protects occupying apartment-owners against landlord owners who are unlikely to be as considerate as they should be, by forcing those landlords to present a copy of the house rules to the tenant, together with the lease, and having the new tenant sign an agreement to comply with the established house rules when they move in.

Other changes in the legislation include an alternative route to dispute resolution and recovery by introducing mediation in the first instance. Where litigation proves necessary, this legislation changes the relevant jurisdiction for management company disputes from the High Court to the District Court or Circuit Court, depending on the value of the claimed dispute. The effect of these changes is a more accessible way for apartment-owners to challenge errant developers or ineffectual management companies.

One of the significant changes introduced by this legislation varies the management company's position under established company law by providing that, unlike other companies, a management company cannot be struck off for failing to file an annual return with the Companies Registration Office (CRO) for a longer period. The previous time limit was a year, which has now been extended for up to six years. This caused apartment owners significant problems in the past and hindered sales for many, so this will offer welcome relief, particularly as it applies to existing developments as well as future ones.

By way of caution, buyers are advised that complexes that are comprised of a mix of residential and commercial (retail or office) may be excluded from certain provisions, so it is recommended that the buyer investigate the management company thoroughly prior to signing contracts. This is generally done through the conveyancing solicitor.

Priory Hall

Above is the theory of the MUD legislation. Unfortunately, the reality may be very different, as residents of the Priory Hall apartment complex in Dublin are finding out to their detriment. All residents, most of whom had been living in the development since 2007, had to be removed from their homes in late 2011 over fire safety concerns. The local authority, Dublin City Council, sought to have remedial works carried out by the developer. The High Court subsequently ordered the developer Mr. McFeely, to carry out works to remedy the defects and make safe the development. But Mr. McFeely failed to comply and, despite his passport being in the possession of the Irish courts, he travelled to the UK using a British passport and filed for bankruptcy there, effectively putting himself beyond the reach of the Irish court system. He then received a fine of €1 million and a three-month jail sentence for breach of the court order, which he has appealed.

At the time of writing, there is tremendous support for the owners and residents of Priory Hall and their plight. However, there does not appear to be any method of enforcement against the developer that will make right the financial loss suffered by the owners of these apartments. The matter will be heard before the

Supreme Court in late April 2012 and the outcome will have a huge impact on the apartment market nationwide.

It would be naive to consider this an isolated case. The likelihood is that Priory Hall is merely the first of many and the State will need to provide some form of redress to owners in such cases where the developer is declared bankrupt.

KEY POINTS FROM CHAPTER 22

❖ Conveyancing is the term used to describe the legal process between two parties whereby property is bought, sold, transferred or re-mortgaged.

❖ Any buyer who finances their purchase by way of a mortgage is required to engage the services of a member of the Law Society of Ireland, a solicitor, to deal with the conveyancing.

❖ The legal process is as follows:
  o Agreement is reached between buyer and seller
  o Contracts for sale are issued
  o Signing of contracts for sale
  o Seller now completes the contract
  o Cheque requisition
  o Closing and exchange of keys and funds
  o Registration.

❖ New legislation relating to multi-unit developments will improve the rights of apartment owners.

Appendix 1

GLOSSARY OF TERMS

Advised minimum value (AMV): The auctioneer's true opinion of the value of the property going forward to auction.

Annual percentage rate (APR): The total cost of credit to the buyer, expressed as an annual percentage of the amount of credit granted.

Annuity: Fixed payments paid at regular intervals over a specified period. These are usually made after a period of investment which has helped create or purchase the annuity.

Appraisal: An estimate of the price achievable for a property for marketing purposes, which is not a valuation.

Appreciation: An increase in value in a property.

Approval in principle (AIP): A letter from a mortgage lender outlining how much can be borrowed.

Arrangement fees: Fees charged to arrange a loan on certain products. Usually applied to loans where a special interest rate applies – for example, fixed or capped rates.

Arrears: The total of late or overdue payments for a mortgage or any other regular payment.

Asking price: The initial starting price at which a seller is looking to sell their property.

Asset: Any form of property owned by a person, including currency, stocks and enforceable claims against others.

Assignment: The transfer of ownership of an insurance policy or lease.

Auction: The procedure by which a property is purchased through competitive bidding on the open market.

Auctioneer/estate agent: An individual or organisation who on their own behalf or on behalf of their organisation holds a license to practice under the *Auctioneers and House Agents Acts, 1947–1973.*

Base rate: This is commonly used to refer to the mortgage lenders' standard variable rate.

Bid: An offer of a specific amount of money in exchange for a property, as in an auction.

Bidding: A purchasing process where offers from different parties are communicated to the vendor for their consideration.

Booking deposit: A deposit (typically €5,000 but negotiable) paid, usually to the vendor's estate agent, in an intended purchase of a property. The deposit remains refundable to the purchaser until contracts are signed.

Break clause: This gives the tenant or landlord the right to terminate a tenancy agreement, under specific circumstances, before the date it is officially due to end, and usually requires written notice.

Bridging loan: A short-term loan commonly used to cover or 'bridge' the overlap between the purchase of a new property and the sale of an old one.

Building Energy Regulations Certificate (BER Cert): The official assessment of the property's energy use, mandatory for all properties now offered for sale or rent.

Building insurance: An insurance policy, covering the structure of the building, which pays the cost of repair or rebuilding in the event your property is damaged or destroyed. Any mortgage lender will require their interest in the property/home to be noted on the policy.

Buyers' broker/Buyers' agency: A professional acting on behalf of the buyer exclusively to source, negotiate and acquire property. May include professional house-hunters.

Buy-to-let mortgage: A type of mortgage specifically designed for investors buying a property with the intention of letting it out.

Buy-to-let: Usually an investment property bought to rent out to a tenant.

Capital Gains Tax (CGT): A tax on profits or gains arising upon sale of investment property.

Capital: The amount of money either put into buying a property or the deposit placed on a property – the buyer's own resources as distinct from any loan from a bank.

Capped rate mortgage: This is a mortgage where the interest rate is fixed at a particular interest rate for a period of time.

Caveat emptor: Latin for 'let the buyer beware'.

Chain: In property terms, this is the situation that occurs when a buyer is reliant upon completion of the sale of their existing property in order to complete the purchase of a new one.

Closing date: The date specified in the contract for the sale for completion by paying the balance of the monies due and handing over ownership and possession of the property.

Collateral: Property or other assets that are acceptable to a financial institution as security for a loan.

Commission: A payment received for conducting business.

Common areas: Areas of land or buildings, such as gardens, hallways, recreational facilities and parking areas, where more than one resident shares access.

Completion: This is when all the legal documents between purchaser and vendor have been signed and full ownership and occupation has been legally transferred to the purchaser.

Conditions of sale: Contained in the contract for sale.

Contract deposit: Money paid when contracts are exchanged, usually 10% of the purchase price. In the event of a booking deposit having been paid already, it is normal that a balancing payment is made to increase the sum to 10%.

Contract for sale: Agreement to buy or sell. Prepared by the vendor's solicitor setting out a legal description of the property to be sold, an indication as to how the vendor has come to own the property, and any special conditions relating to the sale.

Conveyancing: The legal process whereby the title in property is transferred from the vendor to the purchaser so as to ensure that the purchaser obtains a good and marketable title, together with all the rights that he needs to own and occupy the property.

Covenants: Rules and regulations governing the property, contained in its title deed or lease.

Credit check: A check is made on the credit history of an applicant, usually through the Irish Credit Bureau, to reveal their history of credit card repayments, outstanding debts, arrears and any court judgments.

Credit history: A record of an individual's or company's past borrowing, including information about late payments and bankruptcy.

Deed: A legal document that shows who owns the property.

Deeds release or discharge fee: The fee charged by lenders at the end of a mortgage term to cover the administrative costs of transferring the property ownership documents to the borrower.

Deferred payment: An agreed short break from repaying the mortgage, usually at a time of high or one-off expenditure.

Deflation: A situation in which prices are falling (the opposite to inflation).

Deposit: A sum of money (usually four to six weeks' rent) paid by the tenant prior to moving in.

Depreciation: The decline or reduction in the value of a property caused by changes in market conditions (the opposite of appreciation).

Detached: A term used to describe a property that stands alone, separate from all others.

Development: A newly-built residence or an older property that has been refurbished and modernised.

Dilapidations: Any disrepair or damage to a rented property. The costs of dilapidations are usually recovered from the deposit.

Disbursements: Expenses incurred by your solicitor while handling a conveyance on your behalf.

Discharge: Paying off a mortgage.

Draft contract: Preliminary, unfinalised version of the contract for sale. Contracts may be considered as draft until such time as they are signed.

Endowment mortgage: Interest-only repayments combined with monthly premiums into an endowment policy designed to pay off the loan at the end of the term.

Equity: Value of the property net of the mortgage.

Excess: The initial sum paid on an insurance claim.

Exchange of contracts: When the vendor returns a signed contract back to the purchaser, creating a binding situation between them.

Fixtures and fittings: Contents which a vendor may include with the sale of the property. Usually, items which are fastened to the property are regarded as going with the property.

Freehold: Where the owner of the property also owns the land on which it is built.

Gazumping – This is when a seller accepts a higher offer from a third party on a property that they have agreed to sell to someone else prior to exchange of contracts.

Gazundering: When a buyer reduces his agreed offer prior to exchange of contracts.

Ground rent: Annual charge levied by the freeholder to the leaseholder.

Guarantor: The lender sometimes may require a borrower to appoint a guarantor, someone who undertakes to pay the borrower's debt if the borrower defaults.

HB47 certificate: Issued by HomeBond confirming that the property address on the certificate has been registered and is covered under the HomeBond Guarantee Scheme.

Homebond: A building guarantee by the National Housing Building Guarantee Scheme offered to purchasers of new homes by the Construction Industry Federation. It lasts for 10 years and covers major structural defects.

Housing index: An index that measures house price movement.

IAVI: The Institute for Auctioneers and Valuers in Ireland, a national body representing auctioneers and valuers.

Inflation: The general rise in prices over time.

Interest only: A mortgage where the borrower only pays interest on the outstanding capital amount owing on the mortgage.

Inventory: The list of contents provided to a tenant who is renting a residential property.

Investment property: A building that is let out to tenants.

Joint tenants: A form of ownership for two parties whereby, if one of them dies, their share of the property automatically transfers to the remaining party, giving them full ownership, irrespective of the terms of the deceased owner's will.

Land Registry: The State authority responsible for the registration of certain types of title in Ireland, now part of the Property Registration Authority.

Landlord: The owner of property that is rented.

Lease: A written contract between a landlord and a tenant that sets out the conditions by which both parties agree to the renting of a property.

Leasehold: A type of ownership in which a person owns a property, but not the land on which it is built. The owner of the freehold will grant a lease on the property for a specified length of time, in return for payment of ground rent.

Legal charge: A mortgage on the property.

Lender: The party, typically a bank, building society or mortgage company, offering the loan.

Lessee: A person who takes a lease from a lessor or landlord for a term of years subject to certain covenants and conditions.

Lessor: A land-owner who leases out his land to a lessee for a term of years subject to certain covenants and conditions.

Listed building: A building officially listed as being of special architectural or historic interest, which cannot be demolished or altered without prior (local) government approval.

Loan offer: The formal letter received from a lender, outlining the terms and conditions attached to a loan/mortgage offer.

Loan to value (LTV): The proportion of the value of the loan to the value of the property on which it is secured.

Maintenance/service charge: An annual charge payable to a management company to administer, maintain and repair the communal areas of an apartment complex or a housing development that has not been taken in charge by a local authority.

Money laundering requirement: The taking of copy identification to comply with the provisions of the *Criminal Justice Act, 1994*.

Mortgage deed: The legal document that confers ownership or title to a property.

Mortgage protection insurance: An insurance policy that covers your mortgage repayments if you cannot repay same, due to illness or redundancy or any other specified circumstances.

Mortgage rate: The interest rate charged by the lender on the amount of the mortgage loan.

Mortgage term: The agreed duration in terms of years for the repayment of a mortgage.

Mortgage: An amount of money advanced by a lender, such as a bank or building society, on the security of a property and repayable over a long period.

Mortgagee: The lender of a mortgage (bank or building society).

Mortgagor: The borrower of a mortgage (the house-buyer).

Negative equity: A situation in which the value of a property has fallen to below the level of the loan secured on it.

Offer: The price that one is prepared to pay for a property.

Payment break/holiday: An option in flexible mortgages that allows you to stop making mortgage payments for up to six months.

Penalty/penalties: A specified charge levied by the lender under certain circumstances, usually for full or part repayment within a specific period linked to a discount, tracker, fixed or other mortgage type.

Pension mortgage: An interest-only loan where the capital will be repaid from the tax-free cash that you can receive from the pension fund when the policy comes to an end.

Peppercorn ground rent: A nominal periodic rent, usually paid annually.

Pre '63: A term used to describe residential investment properties let in multiple units and converted into such prior to the operation of the *Local Government Planning & Development Act, 1963*.

Premium lease: Where rent for the property is paid in full up-front.

Premium: The amount payable for an insurance policy, usually paid in monthly instalments.

Pre-negotiation: The buyers' broker practice of negotiating properties *before* viewing in order to secure greater value. Also used to obtain information on the seller's circumstances.

Principal: In terms of property, the total amount of money borrowed on a mortgage to purchase a property.

Private Residential Tenancies Board (PRTB): A statutory body, established in 2004, with responsibility for overseeing of all residential tenancies, including registration of all leases.

Private treaty sale: The normal type of property sale, where an asking price is quoted by an estate agent on behalf of the vendor.

Professional indemnity insurance (PII): Insurance that a professional must take out to provide cover in the event of professional negligence.

Property management: The management of a property on behalf of the owner.

Property portal: A website that collates properties from a number of different sources such as estate agents.

Public liability insurance: Insurance that covers injury or death to anyone on or around a property.

Purchaser: A person who is buying a property.

Redemption figure: In terms of property, the capital amount outstanding that must be paid back to a financial institution in order to clear an outstanding mortgage.

Refinancing: Refers to the transferral of borrowings to a different lender, usually to get more attractive terms or to raise more capital.

Registered title: Title that was formerly registered in the Land Registry but is now registered with the Property Registration Authority.

Remortgage: Refinancing a property either by switching a mortgage from one lender to another or by taking out a second mortgage to take advantage of any equity gained by a rise in value.

Repayment mortgage: A mortgage in which monthly payments are made to repay the interest and reduce the outstanding capital.

Repossession: When the mortgage lender takes possession of a property due to non-payment of the mortgage.

Reserve price: The minimum price at an auction that a vendor has decided to sell at, having consulted with their estate agent. For understandable tactical reasons, this decision by the vendor is not made public until the auctioneer at the auction decides to declare that the property is 'on the market'.

Retention: The ability of a lender to hold back (retain) part of a mortgage until certain conditions are met.

Sale agreed: The status of a property for sale, when the vendor has verbally accepted an offer from a buyer but contracts have not yet been exchanged.

Search: A request or enquiry for information concerning the property held by a local authority or by the Land Registry.

Section 23: Section 23 relief is a tax relief that applies to rented residential property in a tax incentive area or for certain types of buildings. Relief for expenditure incurred can be set against the rents received.

Section 50: Section 50 relief acts in a similar manner to section 23 above, but specifically relates to expenditure on qualifying student accommodation.

Security/collateral: Property or other assets which a mortgage lender is entitled to sell if repayments are not maintained.

Semi-detached: A property that is joined to one other house.

Sinking fund: The part of the monies collected from apartment owners annually that is put aside to pay for any major renovation or upgrading works that will prove necessary in the future.

Sitting tenant: A person occupying a property who is legally protected against being removed.

Snag list: When purchasing a new home, this is a list of any defects or items that require finishing by the builder. It is prepared by a purchaser's surveyor in advance of closing.

Sole agent: When a seller chooses only one estate agent to sell their property.

Solicitor: A legal expert, a member of the Law Society of Ireland, handling all documentation for the sale or purchase of a property.

Special conditions: Specific terms of the mortgage, usually shown in the loan offer letter.

Specified all risks items: Specified all risks insurance covers specified items such as jewellery, sports equipment, bicycles for loss or theft both inside and outside of the home.

Split loans: A loan where part is on a fixed rate and part is on a variable rate. Two separate accounts are created to represent each portion of the split.

Square footage: A common measure of house size. To convert square feet to square metres, multiply the square feet by 0.0929 to get the square metres – for example, 2,000 square feet = 186 square metres.

Square metres: Another common measure of house size. To convert square metres to square feet, multiply the square metres by 10.76 to get the square footage – for example, 188 square metres = 2,025 square feet.

Stage payments: A loan amount issued in several cheques at different stages. Used, for example, when applicants are building their own home by direct labour and cheques are issued at foundation stage, wall plate stage, roofing and completion stage.

Stamp duty: A government tax applicable to the purchasing price and due at the time of buying property, at rates of 1 per cent or 2 per cent depending on the value of the property.

Standard variable rate: A mortgage lender's standard rate of interest, which may be increased or decreased periodically by the lender depending on prevailing economic conditions.

Structural survey: A detailed inspection of the property that reports on its general structural condition.

Subject to contract: A term that confirms an agreement is not yet legally binding.

Sub-letting: A situation where an existing tenant agrees to sublet some of the property to a third party with the owner's consent and subject to the conditions of the master lease agreement for the property.

Surveyor: A professional person qualified to estimate the value of land and property.

Tenancy agreement: A legal agreement designed to protect the rights of the tenant and landlord, setting out all terms and conditions of the rental arrangements.

Tenancy: The temporary occupation of a property by a tenant.

Tenant: An individual, group of individuals (up to four) or company who holds or possesses property for a time, in return for the payment of rent.

Tender: A sale or letting process usually conducted publicly that requires a prospective purchaser or prospective lessee to submit a bid for the subject, together with deposit cheque. The bidder whose tender is accepted is bound by the law of contract and cannot change their mind.

Tenure: Conditions on which a property is held (for example, length of lease).

Term: A period of time or a definition within an agreement.

Terraced house: A property that forms part of a connected row of houses.

Title deed(s): Document(s) showing the legal ownership of a property.

Title insurance: An insurance policy which a buyer can take out to allow a sale to complete where there is a potential problem with the documentation in proving legal ownership of some part of the land being purchased.

Title search: An investigation, carried out by a conveyancing solicitor, into the history of ownership of a property. The search will check for liens, unpaid claims, restrictions or any other problems that may affect ownership.

Tracker mortgage: A form of mortgage tied to the base interest rate as set by the European Central Bank (ECB) with an additional specified margin (often 0.75 per cent to 1.0 per cent) to cover the risk and administration costs that the lending institution incurs.

Transfer deed(s): The land registry document(s) that transfers legal ownership from seller to buyer.

Under offer: The status of a property for sale, when the vendor has verbally accepted an offer from a buyer but contracts have not yet been exchanged.

Unregistered title: The term used to describe property which is not registered title. With an unregistered title, a chain of ownership going back as far as 40 years is produced giving a 'root' of title.

Valuation: An independent valuation of a property is usually required by a financial institution, to give it comfort as to the security being offered for the mortgage being granted.

Variable base rate: The basic rate of interest charged on a mortgage, which may change in reaction to market conditions, so monthly payments can go up or down.

Vendor: The person selling a property.

Viewing: A period of time during which a property for sale or rent is held open for public viewing.

Void period: A period of time where the property is empty/ unoccupied by a tenant.

Withdrawn: Where the agreed reserve price of a property is not achieved at auction, the property usually is taken out of the auction process; however, it generally remains on the market and available for sale.

Yield: Income from a property, calculated as a percentage of its value – that is, the return on the value of an investment, usually net of purchasing costs. There are various terms applied in relation to yields, each with their own underlying assumptions which should be understood if relying upon a quoted yield.

Appendix 2

USEFUL RESOURCES

Helpful Addresses

Institute of Professional Auctioneers & Valuers (IPAV)
129 Lower Baggot Street, Dublin 2.
Tel: +353 (0)1 678 5685
Email: info@ipav.ie
Web: www.ipav.ie

Ireland Auctioneers & Valuers Institute (IAVI)
38 Merrion Square, Dublin 2.
Tel: + 353 (0)1 661 1794
Email: info@iavi.ie
Web: www.iavi.ie

Irish Credit Bureau (ICB)
ICB House, Newstead, Clonskeagh, Dublin 14.
Tel: +353 (0)1 260 0388
Web: www.icb.ie

Office of the Revenue Commissioners
Dublin Castle, Dublin 2.
Tel: 1890 482 582 (Stamp duty enquiries)
Email: dublinstamp@revenue.ie
Web: www.revenue.ie

Ordnance Survey Office
Phoenix Park, Dublin 8.
Email:
Website: www.osi.ie

Society of Chartered Surveyors
5 Wilton Place, Dublin 2.
Tel: +353 (0)1 676 5500
Email: info@scs.ie
Web: www.scs.ie

Useful Websites

Buyer resources	www.myaddress.ie
	www.propertybuyers.ie
	www.propertyservices.ie
Financial	www.allaboutmoney.ie
	www.financialombudsman.ie
	www.homebrokers.ie
	www.itsyourmoney.ie
	www.redoaktaxrefunds.ie
	www.revenue.ie
Sourcing property	www.4salebyowner.ie
	www.add.ie
	www.adoos.ie
	www.buyandsell.ie
	www.buyersbroker.ie
	www.citylocal.ie
	www.daft.ie
	www.easydeals.ie
	www.ebay.ie
	www.globrix.ie
	www.iavi.ie
	www.ipav.ie
	www.myhome.ie
	www.privateseller.ie
	www.property.ie
	www.propertypromoters.ie
	www.sellityourself.ie
	www.sharedownership.ie

Engineers & Architects	www.architecturenow.ie www.engineersireland.ie www.fahyfitzpatrick.ie www.openarchitects.ie www.projectdesignarchitects.ie www.riai.ie www.scs.ie
Environmental Energy Valuation Agency	www.2eva.ie
Legal Services	www.homebuyhomesell.ie www.legal.ie www.legalservices.ie www.propertysolicitors.ie

'Avoid a Housing Headache' initiative by GDC Ireland Limited

In response to the numbers of ghost estates, incomplete estates and completed estates with no estate management procedures in place, GDC Ireland Ltd. has launched the 'Avoid a Housing Headache' campaign. The aim of this campaign is to promote best practice for those involved in the buying and selling of properties by providing potential buyers with a 24-point checklist, detailing what to expect when considering a newly built home. This will provide the buyer with all the necessary information to ensure he or she makes an informed purchasing decision.

AVOID A HOUSING HEADACHE
Get it Right First Time

What is this campaign about?

This campaign has been initiated by GDC (Irl) Ltd. in response to the numbers of ghost estates, incomplete estates and completed estates with no Estate Management procedures in place. We want to educate homeowners on what they should expect when buying a home. We have created a 24-point checklist which we believe should become part of the national psyche.

We cannot change the past but we can influence the future!

GDC (Irl) Ltd prides itself in excellence in home design. We create homes and a way of life and not just houses.

How can I follow this campaign?

We are inviting the public to use our 24-point checklist when searching for a new home, especially everyone involved in the buying and selling process. If the answer to any of the 24 questions is NO, the Purchaser should satisfy themselves as to the implications of this, so they potentially *Avoid a Housing Headache.*

Avoid a Housing Headache will be promoted nationwide on all our social media platforms, our website, through PR campaigns and in all our advertising.

www.facebook.com/gdcirl
www.facebook.com/avoidahousingheadache

www.twitter.com/gdcirl

www.gdcirl.blogspot.com

For more information visit our website: www.gdcirl.com

Who is this campaign aimed at?

We want home buyers, developers, sub-contractors, management companies, estates agents and solicitors to know exactly what boxes should be ticked in the buying and selling of a home.

We are inviting key partners in the industry along with the general public to help make this camapign viral. We want you to share our message and help encourage, inspire and entrust home-owners with the information they need to *Avoid a Housing Headache and Get it Right First Time!*

How will you promote it?

This initiative must reach the public because we want them to become champions and ambassadors of the campaign. By using modern marketing tools we will drive *Avoid a Housing Headache* via social media. We hope that you will also use your own web and social media platforms in driving this forward...

Facebook
- 1.7 Irish Facebook users; 847,000 daily Facebook users
- 55% Male; 45% Female
- 27% over 35 years; 25% 25-34 years; 91% over 18 years

Linkedin
- 25,000 Irish LinkedIn users

Twitter
- 250,000 Irish Twitter users

YouTube
- 125,000 Irish users
- Second biggest search engine in the world after Google

Forums/Discussions Boards
- Boards.ie January 1 to April 13, 2010: 5.1 million visitors

How can I get involved?

1. Add the campaign banner to all your publicity material
2. Add the campaign banner and checklist to your website
3. Add the campaign banner and checklist to your social media platforms
4. Include the campaign banner on press advertising
5. Inform and educate clients, partners and enquiries via your office of our campaign
6. If and when you get involved we will add your logo to all our platforms so you get recognition for partnering in this campaign

For more information and advice, contact us today!
A: GDC (Irl) Ltd, Kilderry, Muff, Co. Donegal, Ireland
T: 074 9384700 | F: 074 93 84705 | E: gdcl@iol.ie | W: www.gdcirl.com

AVOID A HOUSING HEADACHE
Get it Right First Time

"24-Point Get it Right First Time Checklist"

The Property

- Are the properties covered by the 10-year Homebond guarantee or an equivalent guarantee? [Yes] [No]
- Has the property been certified, by a suitably qualified person, as being built in compliance with the relevant building regulations? [Yes] [No]
- Has the property been certified, by a suitably qualified person, as being in compliance with all the conditions of the planning permission? [Yes] [No]
- Has the property been constructed to a high standard using skilled craftsmen? [Yes] [No]
- Has the property been constructed using traditional materials and methods? [Yes] [No]

The Development & Management Company

- Are the open areas in the development completed and maintained to a high standard? [Yes] [No]
- Is the infrastructure of the development completed and maintained e.g. sewage systems, footpaths, roads, street-lights? [Yes] [No]
- Are you satisfied that there aren't a high number of properties for re-sale within the development? [Yes] [No]
- Has the street-lighting been approved by the ESB and adopted by the local council? [Yes] [No]
- Are you satisfied that the development is complete or active and isn't a ghost estate? [Yes] [No]
- Is it a condition of each and every purchaser's contract that you become a member of the Management Company on signature of the contract? [Yes] [No]
- Is the Management Company operated by a professional and pro-active Management Agent? [Yes] [No]
- Does the Management Agent provide annual budget and expenditure records on behalf of the Management Company? [Yes] [No]
- Does the Management Agent file accounts on behalf of the Management Company in accordance with Company Law? [Yes] [No]
- Are the entrance walls / railings regularly painted and maintained? [Yes] [No]
- Is the grass cut, litter collected and weeds controlled in the public areas on a regular basis throughout the year? [Yes] [No]
- Does the Management Company have public liability insurance cover for the public areas in the development? [Yes] [No]
- Is there provision within the management fee for maintenance of mechanical plant or equipment i.e. pumping stations, sewage treatment plant, children's play area? [Yes] [No]

General

- Is the development situated in a good quality location? [Yes] [No]
- Are you aware of the ownership profile of the development i.e. what is the ratio of owner occupiers to investors? [Yes] [No]
- Are there any independent mortgage advisors available to assist with any financial queries? [Yes] [No]

The Developer

- Has the Developer got an active and dedicated staff of professionals to deal with your queries? [Yes] [No]
- Does the Developer have a reputation in offering a good level of after sales service? [Yes] [No]
- Has the Developer got a reputation for completion of their developments to the highest standard? [Yes] [No]

If the answer to any of the above 24 questions is NO, the Purchaser should satisfy themselves as to the implications of this, so they potentially *Avoid a Housing Headache*.

f Facebook: GDC (Irl) Ltd | Avoid a Housing Headache
Twitter: gdcirl
Blogger: www.gdcirlblog.blogspot.com

For more information and advice, contact us today
A: GDC (Irl) Ltd, Kilderry, Muff, Co. Donegal, Ireland
T: 074 9384700 | F: 074 93 84705 | E: gdc@iol.ie | W: www.gdcirl.com

INDEX

OAK TREE PRESS

Oak Tree Press develops and delivers information, advice and resources for entrepreneurs and managers. It is Ireland's leading business book publisher, with an unrivalled reputation for quality titles across business, management, HR, law, marketing and enterprise topics. NuBooks is its recently-launched imprint, publishing short, focused ebooks for busy entrepreneurs and managers.

In addition, through its founder and managing director, Brian O'Kane, Oak Tree Press occupies a unique position in start-up and small business support in Ireland through its standard-setting titles, as well training courses, mentoring and advisory services.

Oak Tree Press is comfortable across a range of communication media – print, web and training, focusing always on the effective communication of business information.

Oak Tree Press, 19 Rutland Street, Cork, Ireland.

T: + 353 21 4313855 F: + 353 21 4313496.

E: info@oaktreepress.com W: www.oaktreepress.com.